Becoming Earthwoman
Thank You Notes from a Grateful Guest

a memoir of ten years

By Claire L. Dunphy

To Hannelore with love and admiration

Claire

Becoming Earthwoman: Thank You Notes from a Grateful Guest
Copyright© 2018 by Claire L. Dunphy
Design Copyright© 2018 by Dan Roth, Athens Creative Design

Bilbo Books Publishing www.BilboBooks.com
bilbobookspublishing@gmail.com

ISBN 978-1-7326180-2-2

Printed in the United States of America
All rights reserved. Published in the United States of America by
Bilbo Books Publishing. Athens, Georgia

Table of Contents

For my Daughters
Deirdre and Madeleine
and
Granddaughters
Lucy and Gwen

and Friends of the Road

CLAIRE L. DUNPHY, AUTHOR AND ARTIST

The true human can tune to the voice of the river and give it expression.

The true human can tune to the voice of the wind and speak the words that the wind cannot speak without human tongue. The true human can blend with the essences of the forest, the spirits of the rain, the spirits of every creeping, crawling, living thing and can represent them fairly and evoke from them the best that they can be.

– Ken Carey, *Return of the Bird Tribes*

Introduction

*I*n writing this memoir I often thought about adventure, its nature and meaning in our lives. I think we long for adventure most often when we feel stifled by the routines in life and hunger for a change and the stimulating challenge of the new. Personally, I was thrust into adventure by radical changes in my life and was transformed by it. It helped me to realize more of my potential as a human being. Its challenges renewed my faith in the wonder, beauty and meaning of life. If this can happen to me, it can happen to you too.

Frankly I need adventure to be happy. Fortunately life seems eager to engage me in adventure. I find it in exercising my curiosity, learning something new, walking a street in my town where I haven't been before. I find it in helping someone, in the practice of concentrated listening and of course, in reading a good book. I believe *Becoming Earthwoman* will be an enriching adventure for you.

Eagle Feather

On a chilly moonless night in Minneapolis I received an eagle feather. Joe Geshick, a Native American man I'd met only an hour before, gave me the feather. He gave it to me in a dimly lit parking lot behind a rundown café in the Indian part of town. This silky feather clung to my fingers like a breath of hope. I was speechless. I never imagined receiving such a gift.

When at last I murmured, "Thank you, Joe, thank you," the air around us moved. Joe looked at me with a questioning expression on his face. He started to speak, hesitated, then said nothing.

How could I know that when I accepted this feather, I was agreeing to leave my life behind and journey into a new one?

That was 1988 and I was a painter in the city I loved and where I was born, New York City. My studio was a duplex in a renovated furniture factory on a rare industrial street on the Upper East Side of Manhattan. It was redolent with the aromas of bleach, chocolate, and gasoline, a concoction I savored. Unlike my former studio this one had heat, although in the former one I could go to the movies free because it was on the top floor of the old Loews Orpheum movie theater on 86th St. When I moved the theater manager gave me the word "AND" in big red letters from a movie title on the marquee of the theater. I have always believed it is more an "and" world than a world restricted to "either/ or." While this is my firm belief and I was always willing to consider new ideas that could open new paths in life, I was unaware of the startling new journey that soon awaited me. I hung that big red "AND" on a wall at the entrance of my new studio and I turned the top floor into an "alternative space," never imagining that an eagle feather would later open the door to an alternative world of drums, ceremony and animal spirits!

As an alternative space my studio gave many artists I knew a chance to show their work and more exposure to my own work on the lower level. At that time, I was captivated by the colorful energy - charged streets of the city and created many paintings and drawings of the marathon, street fairs, parades, and outdoor markets. All of this work was a celebration of the vibrant city life I loved.

And I loved paint and painters. There was still quite a lot of excitement about art in those days. Art wasn't yet so much about money and celebrity but more like an adventure in space, both inner and outer, that needed to be shared.

Our collective enthusiasm and faith in the importance of art was expressed in a rubber stamp we made. It declared, "Art Saves Lives," though it couldn't stop AIDS, which had just descended on New York like some mythic monster from a Japanese horror film. Transfixed and bewildered, everyone struggled to identify it and bring it to a halt.

No one knew what AIDS was in the eighties. It is hard to believe now that we even imagined AIDS could have been caused by "poppers" in the dance clubs. The term "immune system" was unheard of. When we learned AIDS was fatal, a fearful hush fell over our lives.

The beautiful young actor, Eric, who lived with me, was diagnosed with AIDS. We didn't know where to turn for help. No one did. It seemed we lived in a constant state of emergency. Every time the phone rang we wondered who might be calling with bad news.

Eventually we became involved with herbal medicine, and acupuncture, restricted diets and psychic healers. A friend even got us an audience with the Dalai Lama's physician. We learned a lot that was valuable, but nothing could change the course of this cruel disease. There were no drugs for it then. I told Eric that I believed I had enough money to hire someone to care for us while we were dying which, at the time, seemed a certainty.

When I finally summoned the courage to "take the test" myself, I had my blood drawn. I timed it when I knew neither of my grown daughters would be in town. I had not shared the information about Eric with them nor my fears for myself. I couldn't imagine what I would say to them if the result was positive.

I had to personally deliver the vial to the public health service building on 20th Street. It was the only place in the city where the test for AIDS was being done. A troubled looking receptionist directed me to a refrigerator down the hall. I opened it and stood stunned, staring at the other blood-filled test tubes. No names, just numbers. The interior of that refrigerator, cold, white and antiseptic, made me think of grim cinematic scenes of prison and isolation cells. I shivered. I held my breath. So much desperate hope and fear burned in that cold place and in my heart. Who were those other people in the cell with me? I wanted all of us to be well, to live.

I had to wait six agonizing weeks for the result. I was told perhaps my blood had been lost or there had been a "false positive" as frequently happened then. At last the report arrived. It was negative. I felt a rush of relief and gratitude but grief for those friends whose blood test results were declared positive. Many people I knew died and many were abandoned or disowned by their families, adding to the anguish of that time.

I got to live. But my darling actor did not. He claimed he was infected by a blood transfusion he had in a Chicago hospital and I silently swore off impetuous summer romances, which at first, he had been.

Life was different now. I became more alert, more impassioned, and profoundly grateful for my life. And good at stifling tears at hospital bedsides. I had never seen people endure such suffering or dying, nor had I witnessed such courage or generosity of spirit. The struggle in this dark time of loss and pain to maintain a clear, steady and helpful presence was shared by everyone.

At the same time that AIDS made death a constant companion, the much-heralded Harmonic Convergence occurred. This was an energy shift, a change in consciousness prophesied by Mayans, Hopis, and Hindus, and was brought about by an unusual configuration of sun, moon, earth and planets. It took place in August 1987. The collective prophesies implied it was time to awaken to the needs of the planet and the life on it, or else!

Childhood summers in the country where my mother taught my brother and me the joys of wading in mountain streams, discovering wild strawberries, and listening to baby birds in the nest made me a lifelong lover of nature and a New Yorker who rescued earthworms and ailing birds from sidewalks. I was someone who was aware of the mindless depletion and pollution of Earth's resources and the danger of extinction for many species. This kind of awareness was not widespread among New Yorkers. Though most people I knew in the community of arts and sciences were concerned about the state of the natural world, their concern was without any sense of urgency. The Harmonic Convergence changed that for me, and many whom I knew. It was a "wake up call," one we needed. It even seemed to direct the public consciousness into a slightly adjusted course. "Environment," "endangered," and "ecosystem" were words I saw and heard more often. Many, including myself, began to seek knowledge and inspiration from Native America whose ancient cultures traditionally honored the life of the planet. For me, access to these cultures was confined to books until Joe Geshick scowled at me from a booth in that Minneapolis café. Although I had agreed to meet him, he didn't appear as someone I would care to meet or know, or imagine as someone who would direct me into the vast land of this continent and its spirit as he did in that crossroads moment in the dark parking lot when I accepted his gift of an eagle feather.

A part of the prophesy connected to the Convergence stated, it was necessary for 144,000 people to "awaken" for the betterment of the planet. "Awaken," in this context, can only mean a change or growth in consciousness. I often wonder how many people were made more aware by the powerful gravitational pull of that unusual line up of planets with the earth. I was most definitely one of them.

Personally, I was deeply relieved when I learned about the Harmonic Convergence because I had begun to have visions. I was seeing things. Now there was a reason for it other than brain tumors. A near brush with death, living so closely as I was within the AIDS crisis, added to a powerful line-up of planets is a certain recipe for visionary activity. Clearly a seldom used aspect of my human consciousness had been stimulated, although I don't think the capacity to see visions is far removed from the ability to use imagination, something I necessarily did each day as a painter. It was exhilarating and a little unnerving to experience an expanded reality.

The frequent presence of AIDS deaths at that time inspired many of us to expand our sense of life and imagine existence beyond the physical realm into the spiritual. It was a period of growth and vision for many. The menace of AIDS, its suffering and death, coupled with the Harmonic Convergence, and its warning yet hopeful prophesy, seemed to be shouting, "WAKE UP!!" Wake up, you are alive, you share the amazing gift of life on a living planet, take care of it, take care of yourselves. The image of Norman O. Brown, author of *Life Against Death* comes to mind. He would get on his knees before the filled lecture hall at UCSC and literally beg the young to learn!

The AIDS crisis left us feeling helpless. The Harmonic Convergence brought an inspired sense of purpose and possibility.

I was not entirely a stranger to sight beyond immediate reality. I had all but forgotten a visionary experience more than twenty years before. It occurred when I was a young mother living on 34th Street. Early one morning while looking out the window of my apartment at the inner block I was astonished to see the familiar cityscape of chimneys and other inanimate objects quivering with energy. Everything seemed alive. I wasn't frightened but felt I had been presented with an unexpected gift. Later that same day I put my two little daughters in their stroller and went like a homing pigeon to an art supply store I'd noted around the block. I bought two small canvas boards and my first brushes and oil paints. As an Art History major at Wellesley College, I had been trained to be a dedicated observer. All of that looking and analyzing was an aspect of seeking and questioning which, I believe, led me to this moment in time when, in a sense, I took action. My first paintings were black, white, and red with fast moving lines, reflecting the jolt I had experienced from that vision on an early November morning. After that, I settled down and began to learn how to paint and draw at the Art Students League and never turned back. Nor did I give a thought to that vision again until much later when recalling visionary experience during the time of the Harmonic Convergence.

Visions are like dreaming while awake. Their quality is what Clement Greenberg, the art critic, once said to me about recognizing a good painting. He believed a painting of interest creates the same sensation you have when walking down the street and unexpectedly see yourself in a mirror, the image is familiar but oddly strange. This is how visions seemed to me, familiar yet altered.

The schematic, logic oriented structure of a New England education at no point suggests the possibility of visions entering a normal person's life and so, in spite of what

I had experienced as a young mother more than twenty years before, I was not prepared for what I saw as a guest in a hotel in Vieques, Puerto Rico. Returning to my room one evening after supper I found a tarantula waiting on my doorstep. It looked friendly, almost appealing. I stooped to look at it more closely. Suddenly a hotel staff member came up behind me and said, "I'll get rid of that" and instantly crushed it. I ran in my room, sat on the edge of my bed and sobbed. I felt terrible. I was surprised by the anguish I felt.

Moments later, just as suddenly as the tarantula had been killed, I "saw" a vision of the Earth. The Earth appeared as a luminous globe, a radiant and tender world suspended among stars. Of course I had seen the photos of Earth taken from the Moon but this was strangely more powerful. It shone with arresting iridescence. I saw a living being. I saw the Earth was alive. As I gazed into this startling vision, a spider web of light slowly formed around the Earth. Could this have suggested the web the Internet became or something else? Could it have something to do with the tarantula? Then I had a powerful sensation of the planet beneath my feet. My feet even tingled with vibrations from the ground. I knew profoundly that I was standing on a living being. A warm wave of love enveloped me. I felt a deep love for the Earth. I felt the devotion of a child for its mother. I experienced intensified love for all that I cherished upon the Earth, and I felt loved in return.

Later that night as I repeatedly recalled this vision and could find no words to adequately describe it to myself or truly understand it, I tried to imagine how I could possibly put this magical earth on canvas. And finally, giving up, I just playfully imagined myself as a character named Earth Woman bedecked in green sparkles and sequins orbiting the planet as a way of embracing it.

It seemed the Earth was in some way speaking to me and indicating I had much to learn and work to do. And while I couldn't understand precisely why I received this vision, I believed it was valuable and far too compelling to ignore.

Western culture does not ordinarily consult visions, dreams or the stars for guidance outside of the Scriptures or other sacred literature written in the past. Western culture does not accept the validity of visions outside of its own holy books. Neither does it acknowledge or believe in the visions and dreams of indigenous cultures. Interestingly, it was the many visions in the Old and New Testaments that inspired the great visionary Sioux medicine man, Black Elk, to become Christian.

Because I had a fine liberal arts education and lifelong access to New York's wonderful museums, I knew indigenous cultures respected visions and dreams. Hoping for insights into my changing consciousness I went off to bookstores in search of help from Native American writers but there wasn't much available then. I found only *Lame Deer Seeker of Visions*, *Black Elk Speaks*, and the first of Lynn Andrews *Medicine Woman* series. A volume of anthropological studies on shamanism suggested the possibility of an urban white woman of the 20th century having visions was absurd. After the Harmonic Convergence those bookshelves were rapidly filled to overflowing.

A painter whose work I showed in my alternative gallery came to my rescue: Joan Pancoe, a psychic healer. Up until I met Joan I had not even had my palm read or my astrology chart cast, as many I knew, had. Although Joan was as playful and irreverent as anyone I knew and her artwork wildly original, I believed in her honesty, integrity and sincerity. It was another artist who suggested I visit her studio and that, for me, was a very lucky day. She was a wonderful guide and remains so. She helped me to overcome my fear of expanding consciousness and grow. Nevertheless, I still longed to make a fruitful connection with Native America. I was not yet aware that the road to an eagle feather, and what lay beyond it, had already opened.

Wolves

I don't remember why I fell in love with wolves, but I did. Perhaps it was Farley Mowat's book, *Never Cry Wolf*, which surprised and delighted me. Maybe it was also some primal longing to live in the forest or a submerged ancient memory. Everything I learned about wolves seemed admirable and oddly reassuring, born though I was on 110th street in Manhattan. (It's funny to remember I rose in the estimation of my disdainful teenage daughters when they learned the location of my arrival on the planet. This was because a movie called *"Across 110th Street"*, starring tough guy Anthony Quinn was all the rage among their peers.) And there is now no doubt in my mind that it was wolves, despite my origins, that led me to Joe Geshick, and the first of my eagle feathers.

Just before sunrise one morning, I awoke in my sleeping loft on East 85th Street and watched with amazement a large three-dimensional wolf 's head being formed by twinkling white light at the edge of my bed. It spoke, not in words or growls, but with almost pleading sounds. Some years later I heard those sounds on a recording of wolf voices. They were defined by the wolf biologist as the voice of a mother wolf when coaxing her cubs from the den. No wonder I soon hit the road and roamed the continent after years of pacing Manhattan Island; mother Wolf had called her eager-to-learn cub, me. Indeed, less than a week after witnessing this startling and beautiful vision, a friend asked if I was interested in joining her on an Earthwatch wolf–tracking project. Of course I was! I felt the visionary wolf was guiding me into an enchanted world that I wanted, and seemed to be waiting for.

I was just fifty years old. When family and friends asked what I wanted for that big birthday, I responded impetuously, that I just wanted to go across the continent and tell the earth how much I loved it. They surprised me by translating this into a ticket for a luxurious round-trip cross-country train ride. This journey in December was almost like a preview of coming attractions. I'll never forget the lighted Christmas trees glowing in windows across the prairie, animal tracks in the snow as the train climbed the Rockies, or how my cherished actor, Eric, ran along the train as it pulled out, laughing and flapping his overcoat in a comical imitation of a "flasher."

That inspiring journey made it clear that Earth Woman longed to get out on her planet, but needed to be prepared. So I walked over to Third Avenue and climbed the stairs to the second floor office of Taggarts Driving School. In filling out the questionnaire I omitted any mention of sparkling green sequins. Now fortunately, I had the driver's license I needed to join the Earthwatch wolf-tracking project. I received this all-important document because my driving instructor, Tomas of Taggarts, was a prince and teacher extraordinaire. His teaching method was droll humor... "So Clayah waddaya gonna do about da body ya left back theya?" or "Oooh da poor liddle kid!" he would say if I failed to consult all my mirrors before backing up. Or there was that smack on the shoulder followed by, "So wassa matta wich you?" No surprise he had ulcers and we had to stop now and then for a milkshake to cool their heat. I am proud to say he eventually gave me the ultimate compliment—which was that I could qualify as a driving teacher!

The purpose of the Earthwatch project was to monitor the movement of electronically collared wolves in the Chequamegon Forest of northern Wisconsin. The forest service wanted to know how wide their range was. Each expedition lasted for two weeks. Unfortunately, my friend and I were unable to participate in the same time segment, so off I went alone.

I had to summon a lot of courage and confidence to fly to Madison, Wisconsin and rent a car to drive 100 miles north to the house where people in the Earthwatch wolf project were to stay. When I got in the rental car, hyperventilating a bit, I was unable to start it and had to return to the rental desk. Humiliated, I tried to be cool by saying, "I've never driven this kind of car before, is there a trick to starting it?" Actually there was a button to push in order to insert the key. I have driven many thousands of miles since then but that first 100 miles was a triumph I don't forget. Most previous trips from NYC were short journeys with my two daughters or later visiting them at their colleges or homes in California. For me, this was really foreign territory and I was the driver and the guide.

As an artist I was necessarily a loner. The thought of living with five other people (all women) in a house in the forests of Wisconsin was very intimidating. But then I thought, *if we're all interested in wolves we'll have enough in common*, and that proved true. It was a spacious house where we took turns cleaning, shopping and cooking between our scheduled times in a van that contained the radio tracking equipment for locating wolves, not the enemy spies of films. In the van we listened to various beeps coming from the different wolf collars. With triangulation, something I learned at the time and promptly forgot, we were able to locate the wolves on a map. Each of us had to stay up tracking through the night at least a couple of times. We took long walks searching for wolf scat and when we found it had to dissect it to learn what the wolf had been eating. Bear scat too. Once back in NYC I had to stop myself from bending over to pick up dog poop. And we got so used to peeing in the woods that the urge to squat persisted even in the streets of NYC. We also made plaster casts of wolf tracks and I carried one with me for a long time until I gave it to a Crow woman who claimed the wolf was her "guide." No more than mine, I thought, but gave it to her and she reciprocated with the gift of a beautiful piece of Pipestone that later became the subject of one of my paintings.

Best of all was going out at night to howl in the woods and wait for an answer. One night the wolves returned our calls, coming closer and closer. So endearing were the cracked howls of young wolves mimicking their elders. Though they came close, they backed off in the end and we never did get to see one. A local scientist with us said he had once gone into this forest alone to howl and that wolves arrived and encircled him. He got down on all fours and they all sang together before the wolves disappeared into the brush. He said it changed his life. Well, he got to see wolves. We saw poop and paw prints but complain, I cannot.

Photo Of A Bear

The Earthwatch wolf-tracking project was really the beginnir _
planned for the summer of '88. I was intent on returning to Bear Butte, a mou..
sacred to many tribes, on the edge of the Black Hills in the southwest corner of South
Dakota. I had been there the year before for the day of the Harmonic Convergence,
August 17, 1987 in the company of my dear Eric. There was a lot of concern among people
who felt touched by the Harmonic Convergence about where to be on the actual day. In
response to the *Mayan Factor,* a book written by New Age philosopher Jose Arguelles,
there were gatherings at sacred sites around the globe but Eric and I were thinking, "Well,
maybe Central Park." In fact, there was a gathering there. But I knew that wasn't the place
for us and I was looking for a clue. This, I knew, was very important.

It seems that many people of Celtic descent, of which I am part, experience occasional
supernatural activity in their lives. Could be the Harmonic Convergence was just be
"heating up" what was already inside me. I learned early in my life that when things fall off
walls, spring from tables, or jump from bookcases for no apparent reason, that something
or someone wants my attention. My most treasured experience of this kind occurred
shortly after my mother's death. While I was anxiously sorting things relevant to her estate
in a filing cabinet beneath a bookcase I suddenly heard the sound of paper being pulled
from one of the shelves above. A slender flier wafted down. I picked it up and read the
single message printed on it: "DON'T BE AFRAID OF THE FUTURE." I opened it
and saw that it was an old political pamphlet. Naturally I wept at this reassuring message,
which I believed to be from my dear mother and I put it in a frame.

So, that spring before the Harmonic Convergence when I saw something flip out
of a bookcase, my "sensors" were bristling! It was a photo of a big benign looking black
bear gazing soulfully from its winter den. I sensed this was a "clue" but to what, I had no
idea. The image of a bear was firmly fixed in my mind a week later at a cocktail party in
Sag Harbor. When I mentioned my interest in Native American traditions someone said

of hers had just been visiting a medicine man named Martin High Bear, High

 ..R! I got the number of this friend, a woman living in upstate New York and called

 ..er. She told me Martin High Bear often gave ceremonies at a mountain called BEAR

Butte in South Dakota, that it was a mountain sacred to many tribal people especially the

Sioux and Cheyenne. She said Crazy Horse (who became my personal hero) and Sitting

Bull had both sought visions there.

It was just a matter of "connect the dots." Now there was no doubt in my mind where

Eric and I must go for the big day of the Convergence, Bear Butte! At the time, South

Dakota seemed as imaginary as Oz to me, the provincial New York sophisticate. But to

Eric, who was from Nebraska, it seemed a fine idea and a chance to show me his native

land and introduce me to his family and friends in Omaha. I had "met" Eric when he

phoned me at the suggestion of a mutual friend who said I might let him stay a couple of

days in my guest room when he arrived in New York. "Where are you now?" I enquired.

"I'm in Omaha" he replied. "Well, what on earth are you doing out there?" I said with

disbelief in my voice. "It's where I'm from." *Uh oh, whoops,* I thought, then smiled to

myself when an image of the U.S. map from sixth grade passed through my mind. It was

one of those maps that showed the products of each state and there was Nebraska smack

in the middle with lots of wheat, corn, and cows. But the map of Eric turned out to be

more interesting than that.

I was a little uptight about the visit to Omaha, wondering how I would be received,

especially as a woman nearly twenty years older than Eric, but everyone was warm and

gracious. It seemed they all knew Eric had always dreamed of being with an older woman.

How much older was never mentioned.

We stayed a couple of nights at his family's cabin out on the Platte River. Eric had often

spoken of that wide slow moving river and its birds, and I was grateful to share some time

with him there. His family loaned us a car and off we went, Eric at the wheel, as I hadn't yet

won my license. And I do say, "won" because learning to drive in the streets of New York

City is nothing short of heroic! We crossed Nebraska on a diagonal from the southeast to

the northwest corner going through many small towns seemingly evenly spaced across the prairie. Eric was amused by my excitement over the different ways farmers stacked their hay, seldom like the paintings of Monet. And he laughed when I said I thought the windmills were elegant. They are, if they're not a part of your usual landscape.

Our route touched on the rolling Sand Hills, a stunning part of Nebraska that was once an inland sea. There were so few cars on the road that when you met one coming toward you, you raised a finger from the steering wheel in greeting. At first I thought people were giving us a rude "finger" but it was just the camaraderie of the lonesome plains. The vastness of the land was both thrilling and intimidating for someone accustomed to being comfortably closed in by towering buildings.

The strange thing was I felt I had buried memories of this land. Just before we reached the Black Hills I began to cry. I really sobbed. I had seen some smoke rising in the distance and believed "my people" were there. Eric stopped the car and held me. I believed I was returning home after being lost for a long time. Eric, too felt unusually moved. And we both felt high with excitement when we entered the Black Hills and found ourselves in the middle of a buffalo herd. I wanted to jump out of the car and hug them. We arrived at the Blue Bell Lodge in Custer State Park and were given the suite because nothing else was available. It was full of bear and buffalo skins and various heads. I found them sad but just pretended they were all friendly and sank gratefully into a nice soft mattress.

Bear Butte

*I*n the morning we leisurely drove the winding roads of the Black Hills enjoying the beauty of its deeply forested fragrant mountains. We were both experiencing heightened awareness. Everything seemed brighter, almost luminous, and it wasn't just that we had left urban pollution far behind. When the road descended we were abruptly thrust into the wide-open treeless plain of South Dakota. We drove to Sturgis, a small Victorian farm town famous for the huge annual motorbike rally it hosts. It's the town nearest Bear Butte. There we got directions.

We took a dirt road out from the back of town. It wound up a hill. As we reached the other side, we got the first view of our destination, Bear Butte. What a shock! Towering above the flat land prairie it looked enormous. I suppose we had imagined that a "butte" was more like a hill, not at all like this mountain with a peak that appeared to rise up so precipitously. For a few moments we were speechless. Tentatively I said, "Do you really think that's it? Maybe it's further on."

"No," replied Eric, "that's Bear Butte all right but I don't remember seeing a butte like this before. That's a real mountain." With no substantial idea about what to expect we were flustered, our intentions were wavering before us.

"Okay," said Eric. "Lets' pull off up by that lake and rest a minute." I just nodded. Confused and shaken we sat quietly to gather our feelings and thoughts. Silently we gazed at the majesty of Bear Butte, the sacred mountain, standing alone and magnificent against the horizon. Our first frightened reaction turned into wonder, then excitement. We looked searchingly at each other, smiled, and shared a courage-inducing hug. We knew there was no going back and wordlessly agreed to go on. Then laughing Eric said, "I'll say we did it, ... if you say we did it!"

But we did do it. Well, almost. We had a picnic in the little park and camping area at the foot of the mountain where it appeared less intimidating than it had at a distance. Then we drove up the winding road to Bear Butte State Park, passing a few buffalo on the slopes. We went to the visitor center and were told there was a special parking lot for people doing ceremony or spending the night on the mountain. We signed our names in the register and met ranger Chuck Rambow. He told us about the son of a Cheyenne chief who spent a night seeking a vision up top and how an eagle feather floated down to him. My heart was racing with excitement. We were absolutely in the right place for the day of the Convergence! I asked Chuck if he knew Martin High Bear, whose name had focused me on Bear Butte. "O yes," he said, "he was here a while ago but he's back in Minneapolis now."

We parked our car, and with a couple of blankets in hand, started climbing the switchback trail that winds around the mountain to the top. Once on the mountain I felt more sheltered than afraid. There was only one other car in the parking lot, and we met its owner, Marco, on the trail. He said he had been dreaming of bears for three years and had finally found his way to Bear Butte from California to see the dawn of the Harmonic Convergence from the top of it. We were surprised that only the three of us were on the mountain.

About two thirds of the way up, rain began to fall and the sky was filled by dark clouds forming concentric rings. It looked like a tornado might be brewing. We ran down in a hurry and spent the night in the car. But before this retreat both Eric and I had found places on the mountain where we intended to meditate in the morning. Mine was a perch facing east near the top. With my vision of the planet enveloped in a spider web of light still suspended in the forefront of my mind, I had a plan. I would mentally send out beams of light around the planet with prayers for peace and expanding consciousness. In a real spider web there are concentric circles, not just rays. It was fascinating to learn Bear Butte was encircled by concentric ridges no geologist had yet explained. This made my thought-web complete. It was as though the mountain was the center of a web, the vortex from which I could send my prayers as imagined rays of light. Of course those concentric circles formed by clouds the night before only added to my sense of wonder.

Just before dawn to we emerged from the car, damp and stiff but happy, and began the climb to our meditation spots. From my high rocky perch in the east I was in time to see the sun rise at the edge of the visible world bringing a glorious new day. The vast prairie shimmered with light like a magical carpet rolling out in space beyond my feet. Two little pine trees kept me company and reminded me that I was on earth and not adrift in space!

Concentrating, I imagined my prayer rays moving east across the continent, the Atlantic Ocean, Europe, Asia and on. Then I sent my prayers southeast and into Africa, then south through Central and South America, all the time pausing often to focus on any place I knew was troubled by unrest or sickness or that was home to endangered species I knew about. My thoughts included prayers for courage, hope, and peace as well as food and medicine. I visualized my prayers as threads of light traveling around the Earth and simply put, those threads were beams of love from my heart. My newly born Earth Woman persona had found a way to embrace her planet! Those little pine trees were all that kept me from floating away on a cushion of joy.

These meditations occupied several hours. It seemed that Eric and I both surrendered to to hunger at the same time because we nearly collided on the trail where we again met Marco and later Joanie, a teacher who lived with her family in nearby Blackhawk and was a frequent visitor to the mountain. It was a gorgeous day but only a few other people turned up. A Native American couple on the trail stopped a moment while the man reached down, took some dirt and gently smudged it beneath his eyes. He looked up and smiled, "I want to see the way the mountain sees." We didn't speak, just returned his smile, loving the gift of his words. Surely, we agreed, the dust from a sacred mountain must hold its special energy. I hoped my adventures on Bear Butte were just beginning!

Eric and I and our two new friends, Marco and Joanie, went off to Spearfish for a celebratory luncheon, toasting the advent of the new age we hoped for. Later in the day, as Eric and I drove east toward the Badlands, the sky lit up with a fan made by wide rays of light rising from the earth. Though I have traversed the plains many times since then and seen many dramatic skies, I have not seen that phenomenal sky again. It seemed a monumental statement of hope, a heavenly affirmation of change for our beloved Earth. Maybe these wide rays were a manifestation of the concentrated energy of thousands of people in meditation around the world. Oh we were happy, but my mood changed as we approached the Badlands. I felt a growing dread. The Badlands frightened me. It seemed like a vast ruined and haunted city. We took a wrong turn and were lost. Eric remained calm but I had to squelch feelings of rising panic. What was it about these lands that evoked such powerful emotions in me? Did I have buried memories of this place?

Meeting Joe

"Go to the high place," the voice commanded while I watched the head of a bald eagle facing west turn from white to orange, red, and finally, indigo. In this vision it seemed the sun was setting. And while "high place" in New York in those days suggested the Empire State Building I knew I was being told to go back to Bear Butte and stay past sunset into the night. This vision came not long after the sparkly white wolf appeared in my sleeping loft so I said to the invisible whatever that seemed to be directing my life just then, "Okay, okay, I'll join the wolf trackers in Wisconsin, then fly to Rapid City and go to Bear Butte, but since I have to change planes in Minneapolis, I want to visit my friend, the poet, Carol Connolly. Okay?" There were no further comments from the invisible whatever.

Heading out into the Midwest didn't seem quite so intimidating after last summer's trip with Eric through Nebraska and South Dakota. Still, I did smile at the foreignness of it all.

After being in the forest with wolves, it was wonderful to move into the comfort and good times of Carol's home in St Paul for a couple of days. Not only is she a poet, but at the time, she was also on the racing commission and author of a newsy gossip column. She knew everyone in town and probably still does. Her friends were the most politically and artistically "hip" people I'd ever met. All of them knew their political representatives personally as well as being up to date with all events in the museums and theaters. To top it off, her partner Bill was a great entertainer, always charming us with his songs and piano playing. I was impressed and, I admit, a little bit envious.

Tracking wolves and howling with wolves had, I claimed while taking a walk with Carol, sharpened my perceptions. "Seeing leprechauns are you now?"

"No" I replied, "but right now I can see there's a picture in a store window across the street in the next block and I have got to go and have a look at it!"

I was having a moment of telescopic vision and fortunately I accepted it instead of worrying about my eyes. Because what we found was an oil painting of a solitary individual, who appeared to be Native American, sitting in meditation. It was a painting with a strong presence in earthy tones that looked like natural dyes or clays. It had spirit. Spirit had seemed sadly lacking in a show of contemporary Native American artists I'd recently attended at the Museum of the American Indian in New York. I had been seeking some kind of spiritual inspiration there and was disappointed. Most of the work had an institutional look about it as if it were designed by outsiders to express their idea of how Native American art should look.

This painting was another story. It was a potent blast of truth, and there it was glowing from the window of a thrift shop. The shop owner informed me the artist was Native American, an Ojibwa. "Ojibwa," my ears tingled, taking in the name of one of so many tribes I had not yet heard of. The shop owner said, "I'll give him your phone number if you're interested. His name is Joe Geshick." I gave the shop owner Carol's number and told her it was my last day in St Paul.

When we opened the door of Carol's house, the phone was ringing. It was Joe. We agreed to meet at a diner at 8 o'clock that night. I was excited. Something was going to happen. When she heard the address of the diner, Carol said, "Look, Bill and I will drop you off and be back in half an hour."

When we got there, I could see that this was not the best part of town. Most of the people looked a bit desperate and I guessed the man with long black hair hunkered down in a back booth scowling, was Joe. He nodded once in my direction and I was thinking, "*Oh God what have I gotten myself into. Be on time for once, Carol, - early would be better!*" Then I sat down across from this formidable presence whose first words were, "I been to prison." I smiled inanely. I was brought up with a repertoire of social niceties to cover most situations but had no response for this one. Fortunately, I didn't respond with some dopey thing like, "Oh, how nice," but politely thanked him for agreeing to meet me and told him how much I liked his painting. His scowl scarcely relaxed. I guess we were both trying to decide if we could trust one another. I focused on the array of tattoos on his arms. One said, "*Born to be bad.*" I believed it!

Joe was quiet. He squinted at me with tired eyes. He seemed reluctant to pick up the portfolio on the vinyl seat beside him. So I plunged in. I said I hoped what was next to him on the seat was a portfolio and that he would let me see more of his work. He nodded. Then he opened it and that changed everything. What I saw filled me with quiet joy. His images were simple, elegant and strong. I could feel their sincerity and the love he felt for the way of life he drew and painted, always employing those earthy clay colors. His figures appeared to grow from the earth. They appeared holy. Clearly Joe was an inspired artist. Since that time he has had many important shows, one of which was in the great Cathedral of St. John the Divine in New York City. He won awards and designed the covers for an edition of books by Louise Erdrich.

I certainly understood that verbal enthusing was not Joe's style but I did it anyway. I was so grateful to experience the beauty of his world. And happy to see his nice, rather reserved smile.

We talked shop. I mentioned my paintings and my alternative space and I described what I had seen in that show at the Museum of the American Indian, where it turned out he had once had an internship. Suddenly learning Joe had lived a short time in NYC made him seem more approachable yet simultaneously I felt an inner anxiety mounting. While we talked about artists, brushes and galleries, my inner voice was scolding me. It seemed to be yelling; "*This man is a real Indian. Maybe he knows something that can help you. What's wrong with you? You wanted to meet a Native American. This is your chance. Speak up, coward!*" I suppose I was afraid he would laugh at me, at my tenuous belief in visions, or that he would affirm the meaningfulness of those visions and that would compel me to reconsider my sense of who I was. And I also felt shy. Joe had a strong presence, like his paintings. I was at a loss but the pressure to communicate was too much. I had to blurt it all out in spite of my fears and I began by telling him I had come from tracking wolves and was on my way to Bear Butte. And that it was visions that compelled me to do these things. He looked down for a few moments, expressionless, probably trying to decide how much he wanted to say to me or determine if I was a nut. Then said, "I'm a Pipe holder. I can lead Pipe ceremonies, sweat lodges, and I can bless houses." I nodded, remembering something about praying with a Pipe in *Black Elk Speaks*. Then he said, "I been to Bear Butte. I been there with Martin High Bear. He's my teacher." I gasped, of course I did, life had taken me by the hand and led me to this moment of knowing I was absolutely in the right place at the right time, that I was being encouraged to take this journey and that it didn't seem to matter if I didn't really understand it.

I told Joe about the visionary wolf, and he surprised me with a smile, saying he had once seen a wolf in the forest when he was young. He knew the wolf wanted him to follow it but he was afraid. I told him how I'd spotted his painting in the thrift shop window and he nodded, murmuring, "Wolf." I mentioned the vision of the eagle and how it appeared to tell me I needed to go to Bear Butte. "Mmmm," he nodded, paused, and then began talking about the way of the Pipe, a way of respect and gratitude. I felt he was telling me what was most important to him and that he wanted me to know what was true about him in addition to jail and threatening tattoos.

Joe continued by saying that a part of the way of the Pipe was to give little tobacco offerings to the Earth as a means of giving thanks. He said, "You should try it. Your life will get better. Take some tobacco to the mountain with you."

I said, "Look Joe, I'm not an Indian and I don't want to play Indian, and besides, my life is pretty good."

He looked at me then in a way I've come to associate with native friends, a look without expectation or judgment that can only be described as aggressively passive. I wither under this look! "Okay, okay, I'll do it, Joe." I didn't want to "play Indian," I just needed some sage advice and direction from someone who came from a culture that acknowledged the validity of visions. And here I was. I had just received what I needed from Joe and was trying to deny it. Such ambivalence!

Then anxiously, because it meant so much to me, I told Joe the story of the tarantula and how its death seemed connected to the beautiful vision of a living earth and the spider web of light around it. Joe looked very serious, even somewhat concerned. Finally, he said, "My people, the Ojibwa, we believe Spider has the power, the same as the power of Thunder Beings." I waited for more but Joe had nothing more to say. This was all very mysterious to me.

When Carol and Bill returned to the café, they tactfully sat at another booth when they saw how immersed in intense conversation Joe and I were.

Getting up from the booth where we were seated, Joe said, "I want to give you something," and gave that motion of the head that means, "come with me." I stood up and followed him to his car out in the dark parking lot behind the café. It was there he surprised me with his gift of that beautiful eagle feather. I knew eagles were important to Native Americans and that their feathers were known to have power but I hadn't understood the true meaning of that power until Joe told me eagle feathers are believed to carry the thoughts and prayers of the Creator. I was amazed and humbled by this precious gift.

He told me his Ojibwa name was "Eagle With No Feathers." This was because his mother feared the white man's law that no eagle feathers be had or used by the Indians. She thought he would be safer with that name. This story was a small, sad glimpse of how Joe's life had been.

A couple of years later when I was traveling and living in a van where the eagle feather swung from my rearview mirror, a large grasshopper trapped inside ate most of it. When I reluctantly reported this to Joe, he said, "Must be a pretty smart grasshopper now. Grasshopper's probably out there tellin' stories to his folks jus' like you are." Could be!

The High Place

Isaid a regretful goodbye to Carol and Bill the next morning and, wondering if I was still me, I flew into Rapid City. If you want to sound like you know what you're doing, you simply call it "Rapid." I rented a car and was able to start it. This was encouraging! I got on the highway going west from Rapid to Blackhawk to see Joanie, the woman whom Eric and I had met on Bear Butte during the Harmonic Convergence the year before. Her home, up among the pines of the Black Hills is a little piece of heaven. She and her children were very supportive of my plans to spend the night on Bear Butte. Her son, Julio, even loaned me his teddy bear. I got back in my car, trying to appear confident but in fact, feeling weak in the knees as the moment of truth approached. Was I prepared to accept what I might learn on the mountain? Was I even fully able to accept Joe's acceptance of me and his astonishing gift of an eagle feather? Could I handle a night on a mountaintop, something I'd never done alone or otherwise? Was it safe to be alone? I knew all this anxiety was pointless because it was like a rerun with Eric the year before. I knew I was going to do it no matter what. I just had to be brave. I guess I was brave even though it didn't feel that way.

I remembered to turn off at Sturgis, a town I had come to appreciate the year before for its cozy restaurant, Bobs, home of the cinnamon bun of death. Remembering my promise to Joe, I stopped at the local Ben Franklin and looked over the tobacco counter. When I asked, a bit awkwardly, for a pouch of Bull Durham, the woman behind the counter gushed, "Oh, this makes the best poison. You just boil it up and spray it on your plants and it kills whatever ails 'em. But don't spray too much or it might kill the plant." I was confused. I was thanking the Earth with this?

I took that back road out of town again to the top of the hill with its sudden thrilling view of Bear Butte rising from the plains. This is it, I thought. I am giving myself over to a journey I don't understand but my heart longs for it, which I am only just realizing at this moment. Heaven help me!

I drove up the winding road to the Bear Butte State Park Visitor Center and reported casually as possible to the ranger on duty that I intended to spend the night on the mountain. She just nodded and directed me to the special parking lot and campground for people who are there for ceremonial reasons. It seemed everyone thought it was perfectly okay for me to do this crazy thing. It was the first week of September and there wasn't a soul in evidence, just the bent branch frame of a sweat lodge.

I checked my backpack—eagle feather, inflatable pillow, blanket, teddy bear, water, a couple of bananas, a package of Bull Durham, and with no one to save me from myself, I locked the car and began the climb to the "high place."

The trail is beautiful and around two miles long. There are dramatic views of the Black Hills and the prairie with its many shining ponds, called "potholes," scattered across it. Eric had called them "eyes of the land." I began to give little pinches of tobacco along the way giving thanks for the beautiful afternoon, for having met Joe Geshick, for some flowers on the trail, for the sound of wind in the pines, and so forth. The more I did it, the better I felt. I became aware of so much unexpressed gratitude and my heart just filled up. The calls of mourning doves soothed me and helped me keep going. They were always just ahead of me on the trail and it felt like they were encouraging me. Heights are most definitely not my thing. At least I had taken much of the trail the year before and knew how bad it really was, just bad enough to make me feel like throwing up without actually having to do it.

After several hours of slow climbing, with many stops along the way, including a revisit to the meditation spot of the year before and an imagined conversation with a large porcupine that emerged from its den to look me over, I reached the top. Up there I knew immediately I must shed my fears. I had to trust this situation completely or deny the reality and meaningfulness of everything that had brought me to this point in time.

At the top, I felt a powerful infusion of love. Fear became irrelevant. It even seemed absurd. Even though the sides of the mountain dropped precipitously all around me, I allowed my fears to dissipate into the wind. I knew the mountain was welcoming me. I knew my life would have to change and I was not frightened. Whatever it was, I would embrace it. I hadn't known until then that I was ready to accept whatever I might learn about who I was becoming.

As the sun started to settle into the west, I looked down, way down at the Visitor Center below and saw the ranger get in her car and drive off. I was alone on the mountain. I pulled the little blanket out of my pack, sat under a tree, and ate a banana. And thought about the fact that I had never in all my life spent a night out of doors. I'd never even been in a tent or sleeping bag. Now there was nothing between me the New Yorker, and the earth on top of a mountain in South Dakota, a place I had imagined wild and remote. And absolutely all alone—no passersby to ask for help if I thought I was lost. No phones. Far out, no kidding!

The night was crystal clear, the stars twinkled brightly, and a warm wind was humming in from the south. I tried to remain attentive but started to drift into sleep until a voice startled me. It said, "Look up!" What I saw was incredible. There were threads of light connecting all of the stars, as though a vast sequined net had been thrown across the sky. Then the voice said, "It is a membrane." Then I said, without thinking to whom I might be speaking, "I've never seen that before." The minute I said it, I was certain it wasn't true. I was sure I'd always known that threads of light connected the stars. It was as though some ancient memory had been touched. Words like "mystified," and "thrilled" cannot describe my state of mind then.

After the sky returned to its normal beauty, I ate the other banana, leaned against the tree and started to doze but was quickly awakened by the sounds of an animal, most certainly a coyote. Then the most alarming thing happened, the wind stopped, that wind which had been a comforting companion throughout the night. There was sudden, utterly unnerving silence. Then the wind began again, this time coming vigorously from the west. I smelled smoke, lots of smoke. I ran and teetered around the mountaintop looking for signs of fire but thankfully saw none. I imagined there must have been a forest fire in the Black Hills.

The sunrise was a shock. The sun appeared as a red-hot coal burning in a black sky. It was mesmerizing, both beautiful and frightening, and it didn't seem real. What could it mean? Slowly I stood up and, giving tobacco, asked for safety for the mountain and me. Trembling but with a full heart I gave thanks for all that had been given to me this night, then headed carefully down the trail.

By the time I reached my car I really wasn't sure I was still on Planet Earth. The nature of reality seemed altered. I was dazed and I knew it so I told myself to drive very slowly and carefully. I made it back to Sturgis and to Bob's—whew! A lot of people looked up at me when I sat down because I was a new face and they didn't know where I fit in. Neither did I at that moment. Then with great relief, I was grounded by cinnamon buns with slabs of butter. At least that much had not changed. All the talk I overheard at Bob's was about the massive burn in Yellowstone Park and that the smoke had already traveled all the way to Minnesota. That explained the smoke and the black sky.

I drove to Joanie's house in Blackhawk and reported in. Julio was happy to see his teddy bear, and Joanie declared that what I'd seen sounded like "String Physics." I was on a roll, felt electrified and high from flinging fear aside, so I decided to confront my fear of the Badlands. Indeed, its silent and powerful beauty filled me this time with joyous awe.

Baffled, amazed, thrilled, and feeling my life was somehow newly committed to something I had yet to understand, I returned to NYC and the preparation of shows in my alternative gallery.

I wrote to Joe, describing my experience on Bear Butte and then phoned him. He really had no comment and I realized that my cultural obsession with definition stood in the way of understanding what I had seen. To this day I continue to learn from the gift of that night on top of Bear Butte. Joe was a good teacher! I invited him to New York and said I'd pay his way if he would make a small drawing for me. He agreed.

My Home In Nyc

My apartment in New York was a treasure but it didn't start out that way! I left my comfortable high rise on a park with a view of the East River when my two daughters left for school and the child support ran out. No, I couldn't meet the rent on paintings and part time jobs. It happened very fast and I had no idea where to go. I was aching from "empty nest syndrome", which is no joke. It felt like being mid-air with a yawning void below and nothing to hold on to. My children were gone and additionally, I had to leave the home I'd shared with them for the past ten years and all the memories there. I was not prepared for the aching loss I felt and maybe that's not possible.

The trusty *New York Times* came to my rescue. I went to the real estate section and spotted an apartment for sale on East 85th street, not far away from where I was living. It was in a 100-year-old, five-story building, a former Irish tenement and was owned by a savvy Armenian architect. This was 1978 and co-ops were just beginning to appear in the city. The law required that two thirds of tenants had to agree to go co-op, so Harout, the architect, had arranged for most of the tenants to be his Armenian relatives. With a small inheritance from my grandfather and help from my mother, I started the process of buying an apartment on the second floor overlooking the garden below.

Suddenly the garden apartment became available. I was told I could have it, as well as a basement room underneath. I hesitated. I was feeling very diminished. I was in mourning. I felt bereft, that the most important part of my life had ended. My mother had advised me that at my age (early 40's) I should cut my hair. I didn't think I had much to look forward to. When I mentioned to the owner of the "Deli" where I lived that I had to move but didn't think I had enough money to do it, he looked at the diamond engagement ring I sometimes still wore and said, "I'll give you a thou in cash for that." Done! He was helping to smuggle Jews out of Russia. That diamond moved a lot of people!

A man I had been seeing, a zany poet, thankfully persuaded me to buy the larger garden apartment. Edmond breathed life into my grieving psyche. He led me into new adventures in the city and a larger view of life. Edmond called me "Shakti Louise." It was during our relationship the Dalai Lama came to New York for the first time. I had never heard of him but of course Edmond knew all about him. At that time the Dalai Lama spoke only in the Synod House of St. John the Divine, not in the great cathedral where in later years he spoke to thousands. Edmond and I leaned over the balcony of the Synod House looking down on this small, radiant individual. There was an extraordinary lucidity in the air that I have never experienced in any gathering since then. Most members of the audience were followers of Tibetan Buddhism and their collective mindset manifested a clarity that was palpable. In his hands, Edmond held a rather large rock that was special to him. He wanted it to experience the Dalai Lama. He even lifted it to see this great man! In our fear-ridden society now, I'm sure Edmond would be carried off, suspected of terrorism.

Urged on by Edmond, I added a large greenhouse extension off the back of the apartment into the garden, not the smaller one I'd imagined. I took out a wall to open up the living room with its fifteen-foot ceiling and fireplace, turned the small kitchen into a loft bed with dressing room below, restored the old foundation wall in the basement and made it a very snug guest room with bath. Of course this took a several years of endless anxiety, living with constant dirt, dust and fleas that are dormant until excavation begins then spring hungrily into life.

In the middle of this construction mess I suddenly remembered that early in my marriage, my husband and I had been invited to a party in a high-rise building at the corner of 85th street and I had looked down from the windows to see small buildings with gardens and said out loud, "That is how I want to live in New York," and there I was, with a garden and an apartment which eventually resembled a cottage. And it was on 85th Street! Someone must have heard and granted my wish! As the saying goes, "Be careful what you wish for."

Sadly, I soon lost that fine man Edmond, the poet. I give him credit for a lot of inspiration and staying with me as long as he did during a very challenging, unanticipated education in the laborious arts of drainage, chimney reconstruction, cement pouring, and so forth.

This new phase of my life was, at first, very painful going. My children were gone, my supportive lover gone. Then my art studio partner mistakenly sublet a part of his space to a nightmare fashion photographer. At that time, I was still painting in the loft on top of Loews Orpheum but could scarcely make use of my studio. And then my mother died of lung cancer. Greatly saddened, living hand-to-mouth in the dust and chaos of construction with no end in sight, I ran out of optimism. I felt nothing but loss and sometimes wondered how I could face another day. One dreary morning I began crossing First Avenue, which was, in those days, a very fast moving two-way avenue, and I got stuck on the island between rushing cars. I stood there, swaying, thinking how easy it would be to fall into traffic, a quick death, release from pain. But I waited for the light to change and continued to cross. At the corner was a Hungarian antiques dealer whom I had met when browsing in his shop. He was barely an acquaintance but his arms were wide open. He embraced me. Told me how happy he was to see me. I was dazed. It was almost as though he had guessed my thoughts while he stood on the corner and was welcoming me back to the world.

I continued walking along 85th Street and came to the deep construction site of Bremen House, looked down into it and saw a face I had not seen for ten years. It was Tony. Tony, who had been my assigned teaching assistant when I worked in East Harlem for Columbia Teachers College. He was a kid in trouble, and assisting me was supposed to help. It did because the children in my classes loved him. He had a kind heart but was burdened by a severe speech impediment that isolated him from his peers and made him an object of their scorn. I can still hear how he spoke to me then, "Hey-ey-ey m-man." The last time I'd seen him was on Riker's Island when I bailed him out of jail. He was there for possession of a gun. He said he'd been set up, and I decided to believe him. Now here he was in a construction site, ten years later, jumping up and down shouting, "Clara, Clara!"

"My god, Tony, is that you? Is that really you?" I yelled. The entire work force stopped and gaped. Tony raced out of the pit and I ran to embrace him. At that moment my life turned around. It was as though I was being rewarded for opting to live when I had just imagined throwing myself into the traffic of First Avenue to end it all.

Tony brought me the carpenter, plumber, and electrician from this work site. They all agreed to work for me weekends, and thankfully, as I could pay them. They completed my renovation within a year. I had my wonderful home with its garden and struggles, but mostly the joys of it, until I sold it twenty-five years later in 2002. It felt like a miracle. I think it was! The gods do take pity on us from time to time. That apartment, which once resembled a disaster zone, was later featured twice in *Woman's World* magazine only five years after I purchased it in 1978.

I assumed Tony was now drug free and making a good living but tragically he later killed a man. He did it to belong to a gang. Such was the pain of isolation he must have felt. The terrible story of violent initiations for the privilege of belonging is repeated all over the world where there are rootless young men who need, at the very least, decent work, inspiration, and community. Tony is now out on parole after twenty-five years in prison and has been deported to Trinidad where he has family. We remain in touch. He's doing well. He conquered his stutter. And I remain grateful to him, though saddened by the pain he both caused, and experienced.

A Visit From Joe

Smiles did not come easily to Joe Geshick. But when he stepped out of a stretch limo in front of that little apartment building on 85th Street, his face could barely contain the grin on it. Usually I arranged for a car service to pick up visitors from out of town but this service had run out of cars and only had a limo free to pick him up. What a picture he made, that handsome, stocky Indian with his long black ponytail, carrying his fringed deerskin Pipe bag. He looked like an ambassador on a special mission, and in fact, he was just that, an emissary from another country with important information.

He settled into my basement guest room and began calling friends.

As a child I loved going to the old Museum of the American Indian, partly because it was quite a journey up town (a real trip), partly because of the shrunken people (such delicious horror!), also because I liked the feathers and colors, and because my mother thought my brother and I should know about the tribes of the continent. How remote and exotic they seemed. Now my doorbell was ringing nonstop—Cherokees, Mohawks, Apaches, and Lakotas were at my door. Amazing! All those people I thought lived so far away and who seemed nearly mythical were suddenly in my home. Here they were, other New Yorkers complete with New York accents, no longer the occupants of my imagination but real people. Part of me felt like a child clapping for joy while the rest of me was simply astonished. I found out that most of them had attended workshops taught by Martin High Bear. They told me Martin had received a vision on Bear Butte instructing him to help urban Indians connect to their origins and bring the Pipe into their lives. They all seemed in awe of him, except for Rosy, a diminutive Apache woman with flashing dark eyes, a long thick braid, and a Bronx accent. She could make a joke out of anything.

Joe announced he would give a Pipe ceremony the next evening, that friends of his would come and that I should invite friends too. He said my basement room would be a good place for the ceremony, dark and close to the earth. He needed a blanket to put on the floor for his altar, a candle, a glass of water and something to hold the prayer flags. He needed cloth to make these flags so we went to a fabric outlet on 86th Street and bought red, black, white, and yellow cloth, the colors that represent the four directions. It had to be pure cotton, no blends. Joe was very specific. Then we had hot dogs at Papaya King, none better in this, or any world! We visited my duplex studio on 91st Street purchased with an inheritance from my mother. I was working on small paintings of tropical moons and phosphorescent nights inspired by visits to Vieques, Puerto Rico. I think Joe's nods were positive responses though it was always hard to tell with him. When Rosy saw these paintings she said, "You turned your tears into rainbows" and studied me under lowered eyebrows.

Joe made four small fifteen-inch flags, one for each direction. Black was for the west, red for north, yellow for east, and white for south. He cut the material and put tobacco in the corner, tying it off. Then we went into the garden and found some sticks and attached the little flags to those. We stood them in a vase and Joe placed them on his altar for the ceremony.

Ten or twelve people attended. Joe was burning sage in an abalone shell and he smudged each of us by fanning the smoke with a feather, and then we all went down the stairs through the greenhouse into the basement room. Pillows were placed in a circle. Light from a candle flickered over the objects on the altar. A surge of almost painful tenderness rose in my heart when I saw the objects on the altar were all from nature: a deer antler, a shell, a wolf claw, and some small wrapped bundles. It felt like each object was a spirit accompanying Joe to participate in this ceremony. Each had an aura of sacredness.

Joe briefly related the story of the Pipe, that long ago, a beautiful woman appeared one day on the Plains and was seen by two hunters. One of them tried to seduce her and she turned him to dust. She told the remaining hunter to return to camp and prepare a lodge where she would speak to his people. When she arrived at the lodge, she brought out the Pipe and explained for a number of days how to pray with it and live by it. When she left, walking away through the tall grass prairie, she appeared on the horizon as a white buffalo calf. That Pipe, Joe explained, is called the "White Buffalo Calf Pipe" and is still in existence in Green Grass, South Dakota. Joe said quite sternly that the Pipe is not a religion but a way to live, a commitment to respect and honor all peoples and all the life of earth.

When Joe started beating on a drum, portals to another world seemed to open. He invited us to join him in the old Lakota songs that are a part of a Pipe ceremony and then, as he lit his long stemmed Pipe, he blew out the candle on the altar. Only the bowl of the Pipe glowed in the sudden darkness. There was a short gasp from those of us in the circle, and then Joe began to pray in his language. I was struck by the quality of ancientness, of primal authenticity in this ritual, and I felt I was being returned at last to my true spiritual home. I felt, in fact, I had never left it.

Joe allowed all of us to hold the Pipe, pray with it, and smoke it, though he warned us not to inhale as the tobacco was strong. He instructed us that prayers are concluded with the words, "O Mitakuye Oyasin," meaning, "for all my friends and relatives" and reminded us that "friends and relatives" can include other species and life forms, spirits, and ancestors. That this was a spiritual way brought to the Lakota long ago by a woman made it all the more profound and attractive to me.

Although my parents were not churchgoers, they had dutifully sent me as a small child to Sunday School. It was during the War. My beloved uncle was fighting in the Pacific. I insisted vehemently I would not return to that school because I refused to love everyone as the teacher instructed. I could not imagine loving anyone who wanted to hurt my uncle. As a teenager I was curious about religion and attended a number of churches but found no inspiration. In college my secondary interest was Comparative Religions, which was very enriching, but nothing spoke to my heart until Joe brought the Way of the Pipe to my basement.

Some people felt puzzled by the experience of the Pipe Ceremony but for most, it resonated strongly and they left inspired.

Rosy and I hit it off. I asked her if she could lead a Pipe ceremony for women in my home. I said, "We women really need it" I thought we desperately did need this kind of affirmation of our natural desire to preserve and nourish life. "Yeah," was her Bronxian reply. Well, Rosy subsequently led Pipe ceremonies in my home for thirteen years, and our circle grew to include men, people from many countries, and visiting medicine people. After a time, it became known in Native American circles that a Pipe ceremony would take place on 85th Street every New Moon. Rosy brought her Pipe, and I learned to prepare the altar. I made the flags and breathed prayers into the tobacco that I tied into them. Sometimes these prayers would be for the life of the sea, or the forests, or for victims of disasters. I got to choose. And I did the best I could to represent as many life forms as possible on the altar, which was a large red, yellow, and black cloth woven in Burma. People who came added to the altar. All the objects on it reminded us that we share the planet with many other beings. We wanted all of them to be present. We learned the Lakota songs that are a part of the ceremony and other songs in nearly forgotten native languages.

The Room In The Basement

Alot of magical things occurred in that room. When Galen, a medicine man from South Dakota, came to give a ceremony, he told me we would all have to eat a small piece of raw kidney during the ceremony because his spirit guide liked it. This was a hard call, especially for the vegetarians, but we all did it. During the ceremony some of us saw lighted footprints moving across the carpet! Others saw small spirit lights darting around the room.

Rosy was also empowered to give the Mohawk ceremony for the dead on Halloween. During this ritual we spoke to dead relatives or friends. I spoke to my father, with whom I'd had a difficult relationship, and I remember saying that what happened in the past no longer mattered and that I just loved him. I surprised myself in saying this. The following evening, I ran out in the cold to get something from the vegetable market around the corner. An elderly gentleman arrived there at the same time and I opened the door for him, remarking on how cold it was. "Oh this isn't so cold. I know real cold. I went to Dartmouth. That's in New Hampshire."

"Dartmouth," I exclaimed. "My father went to Dartmouth! His name was Henry Richmond."

"Hank Richmond! Good old Hank! My name is Gristede, like all those grocery stores around here."

"I heard some stories about you Mr. Gristede—Red," I added. His reply was rich laughter. Indeed, my father told me Red had once been caught in the showers on a day that girls were allowed to visit the dorm and he wrapped his head of red hair in a towel and ran for it, forgetting that red hair shows up on other parts of the anatomy.

This encounter left me a little wobbly. There was and is no doubt in my mind that my father was returning my "hello" through this remarkable encounter with Mr. Gristede, whom I never saw before or after that night.

Over time, those who frequented the Pipe ceremonies in my basement room noticed changes in the stone wall. The stones became more articulated. It was the original foundation wall of the building and was made from chunks of mica-filled stone held together with mortar made of sand and pebbles. Instead of covering it with plaster as I was advised, I cleaned it up and it was beautiful. It seemed alive. A Japanese friend noticed that a part of the wall had taken on the form of the Japanese character for "cloud," or "spirit." It was as though the stones spoke to us. Some people joked that the wall was the veil between this world and the world of spirit and I joked that the ancient boiler behind the opposite wall was probably the conduit for the magic we experienced there.

That room became somewhat notorious because friends and friends of friends who stayed there overnight often reported unusual dreams or appearances. One friend saw a newly deceased cousin slide under the door to the room, flicker, and fade away. A young man from California who came for the weekend laughed at the reputation the room was developing and awoke during the night to see his shoulder clamped in the jaws of a large wolf. He was terrified! I was impressed!

All that happened there began with Joe. On second thought, I guess I have to say it all began with the mother wolf who appeared to me in my loft. Or was it the photo of the bear and all that it led to?

When Joe presented me with the drawing I had asked for in exchange for a plane ticket, I was so happy to see it included a spider web above an abstract human figure presumably representing me. I am so fortunate to have this drawing. I believed then that it validated me as well as the beautiful vision of the web of light that had so moved me. I needed it because I was not yet secure in my evolving beliefs that were outside the conventions of most people my age. This drawing was an affirmation that I was in a recognizable place worthy of recognition, at least to Joe. I treasured it and always will.

This quotation or variations on it, were often spoken in that special basement room:

"All things are interconnected; whatever befalls the earth, befalls the people. Man did not weave the web of life, he is merely a strand in it. Whatever he does to the web, he does to himself."

Chief Seattle purportedly said this, coining the phrase "web of life." The phrase was widely used at the end of the eighties. Whoever may have originated it, it certainly resonated for me, caught up as I was in so much web imagery revealed to me by the supernatural world as threads of light. Such powerful beauty! The world of immediate reality, personified by the news media, was daily reporting the destruction of webs of life, which eventually became defined as "ecosystems." Thousands of species continue to disappear as ecosystems are being torn apart. How many holes in the web of life can the planet sustain? Our species has rapidly created so many fantastic connection and information webs and devices. Do we intuitively sense a need for web reinforcement, protection, or repair? And there is so much urgency surrounding these connection systems as if to say we must, at all costs, remain connected. Is something about to collapse? Is it collapsing now? I was seized with a sense of urgency! I had seen dazzling, extraordinary things that infused me with wonder and anxiety. Why was I seeing these things? What was I supposed to do? Furthermore, I was sizzling with energy and a lot was going on—friends were ill and dying, there were shows to hang, visits to the psychic healer, paintings to paint, ceremonies, and a re-imagining of my life. I had work to do! But what? I was an artist with a love for the natural world and a growing connection to the mystical that I found irresistible. And so I ended up painting on rocks. Now how predictable was that?

Soon after his visit to NYC Joe called, "I'm gonna be Sundancin' in Green Grass. Friends can come and support me. That's August." This is a good example of an Indian invitation, not very direct and necessary information usually incomplete. To say, "I want you to come" would be too direct, would impose a feeling of responsibility and so would not be polite. It is also assumed that if you are meant to be there you will figure it out. This phone call came in the spring, now 1989, so I had plenty of time to unearth the details. "*Green Grass Green Grass.*" I hummed to myself, "*home of the White Buffalo Calf Pipe.*" All that I had seen of South Dakota so far was puma brown. Was it really green there? I was determined to go. Joe had helped me so much and I hoped I could be helpful to him. Whatever "support" meant, I wanted to give it.

St. Francis And
Phosphorescent Nights

A shrine to St. Francis of Assisi stood at the entrance of the old sugar plantation. It was a large dome-shaped boulder, painted white with a handsome long cement altar resting on top of it, the elegant cement work unique to Puerto Rico. A small statue of St Francis perched on top of the boulder. There was a stone platform built all around it, suggesting it had once been a chapel. It was engulfed by trees, appeared neglected, but radiated a charm that suggested a benevolent past.

The plantation house itself, called "The Casa," had become a small hotel. It was a bit shabby, with an inner courtyard, high ceilings, wide porches, and big shuttered windows opening onto tropical foliage. It had a seductive aura. The owners were a smart, fun, and funny couple from Boston.

Once we'd discovered this offbeat place on the island of Vieques, a part of Puerto Rico, my two daughters and I stayed there a number of times. We could walk to several beaches where we were more likely to see wild horses than other people.

The island also had one of the few biolumenescent bays in the world. When we swam there at night, even the droplets clinging to our eyelashes glowed in the dark. Anything that moved created light: a school of fish dashing into the bay from the ocean or a resting heron suddenly taking flight would set off an explosion of light. Above, was the glorious star stream of the Milky Way. One of the early art installations in New York was a blackened room in which pinpoint lights glowed from the walls, the ceiling, and floor. When you stepped into it, it was like being suspended in space among the stars. This bay on Vieques seemed the magical model for that artwork, with its lights from pulsing stars above and living microscopic beings glowing in the water below.

The tropical nights of Vieques were also adorned by phosphorescent life glowing from tree roots, fungus on fallen logs, even on leaves just outside our windows and all of it was accompanied by a multitude of fireflies.

Irving, the owner of the old Casa, tried to support artistic activity on the island. . He bought some paintings of mine and several became postcards sold by the Casa and the tiny museum in the nearby village of Esperanza where I once had a show of my moonlit Vieques paintings. When I suggested to Irving that I paint the animals of the world on the St Francis boulder, he actually agreed!

I decided I better spend at least one nighttime hour of meditation by the boulder to get a feel for it, in essence to get its permission to paint on it. The first night curled up against its cold hard surface I heard nothing. On the second night I had a sensation of merging with this stone and I heard, "I am so old," and then, "a thousand star songs are locked within me." This was perfect. I was still transfixed by the image of the starry net of light I had seen on top of Bear Butte. Now stars as well as animals would glow from the boulder too. I had strong feelings of connection between this boulder and the mountain. Additionally, I knew stars and animals had long been seen as companions in the heavens. After all, many constellations are named after them.

I planned to return to Vieques the winter following Joe's Pipe Ceremony in my New York apartment in the fall of 1988. I couldn't wait to do the work there. I began making animal cutouts. The surface of the stone was pocked and uneven. In order to make the animal forms recognizable I needed the help of these silhouettes. Soon I had a book full. Making them was a gleeful journey. The wonder and wit of creation is boundless. What human imagination or logic could cook up a living thing as splendid as an elephant or porpoise or dragonfly? All of them perfectly attuned to their environments, perfectly woven into the fabric of life. I placed these silhouettes in plastic sleeves and put them in a three-ring binder. I grouped them according to species or environments. I relished leafing through this binder thick with life, almost chuckling like a Midas over his riches.

When I arrived in Vieques I had already imagined the dome-like boulder painted cobalt blue with the animals painted white, glowing like stars. They would have to be outlined with purple to give them a vibration against the blue. I didn't want them to appear static. The stars themselves would be yellow. Then I imagined a rainbow painted across the dome of the boulder continuing on to the altar. In my mind it was a rainbow connecting heaven, the domed boulder and earth, the altar. The phrase from the Kabala, "As above, so below," stood like a billboard in my mind. On the little ledge that held the plaster statue of St. Francis, I wrote it in Spanish, "Como Arriba Asi Abajo." And I gave that sweet fellow a fresh coat of paint.

First I repainted the boulder and altar white after Irving had it sand blasted. After that I began outlining the animals, adding stars, and starting the rainbow. It was a huge amount of work! I was having severe backaches. Thank heaven another guest at the Casa, also an artist, volunteered to help. If not for Stevie Heller, it would not have been possible to finish. And Stevie was good company, making the experience a lot more fun. He suggested I make a silhouette of Panchita, the charming flop-eared hotel dog, who joined the guests each night on the bar stools for a sip of beer. Sometimes our work was interrupted by wandering horses that visited the altar and one morning we witnessed two young stallions challenging each other in a nearby meadow. I had no idea horses could be so fierce.

Irving announced there would be a ceremony to celebrate the completion of the work. How perfect it was that the priest officiating was a Father Francis! He blessed every animal image with holy water and gave Panchita an extra splash. I was asked to speak and said, as I referred to the boulder and its altar, "Here is a celebration and prayer for the great web of life of which these animals, stars, you and I are all a part. The animals and stars are drawn on the same scale to suggest all life forms, whether bear or butterfly, have important roles in keeping our planet healthy, humming, and happening!" I concluded with a little bow to St. Francis. And then that generous man, Irving, let the champagne flow. Throughout I kept hoping I could use my treasured book of animal shapes again. Later I did, again and again.

Trance Travels And Traveling By Van

Back in New York City, my friend the psychic/artist Joan, was teaching me how to go into trance through a special breathing technique. I knew nothing about trance, soul growth, chakras, the higher self, past lives, Chi, and so forth. And now they were all becoming a part of my new life, along with Pipe ceremonies and Sweat Lodges! As a slightly calloused New Yorker I probably would have made some snide remarks about such things before discovering them myself. It's so often the case you end up becoming what you once sneered at!

Yeah, and I was "into" crystals too. I think the Beatles first opened the door to these Eastern concepts for the populace at large. Then the Hippie epoch took over. I scarcely noticed at the time because I was a young mother of two. Now I had the time, chance, and need to expand my consciousness.

The trance state illuminated some of the reasons behind the direction I was taking and was very useful when I had no idea what I was doing! For me, going into trance was a bit like going to the movies but without the lengthy credits. The special breathing to facilitate the trance state essentially clears the mind of all its habitual chatter. Once clear, there is room for new information to manifest itself. Some comes from outside, some from deep within. What arrives is often very beautiful and always valuable. Returning from trance I often felt weightless as though I had traveled far beyond my physical presence. I always learned something helpful and always felt grateful.

I wanted to return to the Sand Hills of Nebraska. Eric and I had passed through a corner of that area on our way to Bear Butte for the Harmonic Convergence. But why did I feel compelled to return? In trance I connected with a former life in that region. It seemed I left my Native American clan to be the apprentice of a traveling medicine man. I saw the landscape and some of its details and I heard, "Snake River." A cave-like place in a cliff appeared. I felt summoned there for a night of meditation just as I had to Bear Butte. What did I need to experience there?

I knew of the Snake River, a large river that runs through Idaho and Wyoming, but I knew that was not "the one." The atlas I had listed a few Snake Rivers and yes, there was one in the Sand Hills! It was just south of Valentine, and that in itself sounded appealing. I was ready for adventure. I decided to go to the Sand Hills, find the Snake River, and then go north into South Dakota to the Sundance and support Joe. Somehow I would find my way.

This of course meant renting another vehicle and I decided to rent a van, a Dodge Caravan, and try to live in it. I just hoped I could start it.

I flew to Minneapolis and stayed a few days with Carol and Bill in St Paul. Bill took me shopping for my "live in the van necessities," a sleeping bag, foam mat, lantern, binoculars, camping stove, and a cooler which would double as a table and desk for my portable, battery powered Canon "Typestar" typewriter. I miss that trusty machine! It seems there's always some problem with my computer. I also had paints and my book of animal cut outs, just in case. I resembled a kid with a book of paper dolls hoping for a chance to play.

While in St Paul, I visited Joe in his spacious studio in the Rossmore Arts Building. I met Celine there, the former nun who spotted Joe's potential as an artist when he was in prison and smuggled in forbidden art supplies. That wonderful woman also made a habit out of freeing trapped bears. Maybe that was the same thing as giving paint to Joe! She later taught me how to change a tire and insisted that I find an old rug for campsites. If you put a rug down she claimed, you'll always feel at home no matter where you are, just like the Arabs. I found a blue Navajo style carpet, scarcely worn, in the trash on my block in New York. I couldn't believe it was being thrown away. I looked up and down the street thinking someone would claim it, but it was mine. Celine was right. The rug defined my patch of earth wherever I landed. She had an unusual flair for freedom.

Joe had been commissioned to build a sweat lodge on the outskirts of St. Paul. Usually the underlying structure of a sweat lodge is chokecherry branches bent to form a dome. Then it's covered with blankets, plastic, skins, or some combination of these. But Joe used bark and moss to cover the branches. It was beautiful. It seemed to have grown right out of the earth. Joe included me in a Sweat Lodge Ceremony. And oh yes, I was scared when I crawled into that small dark lodge on all fours, crouched in the back away from the little opening to the outside, watching the glowing hot rocks shoveled one by one into the fire pit and when the opening to the outdoors was closed. Water and bits of cedar sizzled on the rocks and the lodge was filled with hot steam that burned my face. Yes, I was scared. I'm often asked if I'm ever afraid and I reply yes, but so what? Fortunately, I do have some common sense.

The "Sweat" was similar to the Pipe ceremony Joe had led in my New York home. Prayers were sung and the Pipe passed around, although more than once. Most powerful were the rocks themselves, their life force overwhelmingly present. Joe's brother, Ray, was the "fire keeper." The first four rocks he shoveled in were the largest and were offered to the four directions. When water was poured on them, they sputtered, they sang, and hauntingly, howled. Spirit faces flickered over their surfaces. I was stunned. Joe smiled.

And as promised, there was a sensation of rebirth when we crawled out of the lodge into a starry night. Wet and muddy, we felt overwhelmed by love from and for the earth, the heavens, and our fellows. Joe pointed to the print in the earth I had made when entering the lodge. It looked like the print of a deer hoof. He had already told me he no longer hunted deer because one had saved him from suffocating during a sweat by pawing an opening in the back of the lodge. He honored the life of deer just as one had honored his. The sweat lodge is a holy place. Good thing I put my fears aside!

Bill and Carol agreed to store the back seats of the van I rented so there was plenty of room for my new sleeping bag and cooler. Celine gave me a bunch of old cooking and eating utensils. Carol launched me on this first voyage by van with a coffee mug that had "Some Leaders Are Born Women" painted on it. I hoped I was worthy. Again I was scared but remembered how I had felt when leaving Joanie's house in the Black Hills to spend the night on Bear Butte. It was the same kind of scared feeling that is also joyful anticipation. But as usual, I kind of hoped someone would save me from myself.

Home To The Snake River

My mother taught me to read maps. I loved them. I liked seeing how places are connected by roads or rivers and I began to have a feeling for how mountains and plains, valleys, deserts, and seas are all woven together in beautiful and mysterious ways. I loved to view the lay of the land. In college I studied geology and later attended lectures at the Museum of Natural History. I hoard maps and can never throw any away. Plotting routes to the Sand Hills, Nebraska from St. Paul, Minnesota was soothing. If you can find yourself on a map, you're not lost, right?

Once I had driven beyond urban areas and was on less traveled roads, my anxiety departed and was replaced with the joy that adventure brings. This adventure began in the rain and I mastered all the speeds of the windshield wipers both front and back—very empowering! I felt I was living up to the slogan on Carol's coffee cup.

Just as the rain stopped I pulled into Split Rock Creek State Park and found a beautiful lake and trees full of goldfinches, doves, redwings, and meadowlarks. I was approached by a man whom I thought was a camper but was in fact a postman who sometimes used the restroom there. I told him I was an artist from New York City and he told me about a painting of his old family homestead done by an eighty-year-old aunt. "Homestead" seldom enters conversations in New York! Next on my map was Pipestone National Monument where the red stone (Sioux quartzite) used to fashion the bowls of Lakota pipes is quarried. This red stone is believed to be "the blood of the people." Because of the rain that day, the colors at Pipestone were very vivid, merging into purple and orange and deep burgundy. Delicate ferns and lichens adorned the crevasses in the stone and there was a stream gently splashing through it all. I recognized the yellow starburst lichens on the red stone as a feature from a vision I'd had. This was both startling and comforting.

I stopped at a restaurant in the town of Pipestone and someone quickly started chatting with me. Then a woman came over and asked, "Are you the artist from New York?" I guess the appearance of an artist from NY ripples through the airwaves in western Minnesota!

They were eager to share what was special about their town, their small museum with its pioneer and Indian artifacts, and the fabulous old hotel, the Calumet, known as the "gargoyle building" though it was named after the Indian peace pipe. Carved stone roundelles on it depicting the north wind, Punch, (that comic figure in Italian puppetry) a lion, and others, were all very comical. I was told that one was so offensive it had to be removed. Naturally I wanted to know what that was but no one could or would tell me. It was built in 1896 from Sioux quartzite.

I continued on to Blue Mound, a beautiful prairie park, where sunlight danced over the tall grasses, sages, and thistles as they swayed in the breeze. The sweetest aroma swelled from the earth. There was a small group of buffalo there, so solemn and vulnerable I felt my heart fly to them. There were rocks there, arranged to somehow connect with the equinoxes, and a cliff that had been a buffalo fall. It all aroused an indefinable longing in me.

I was not yet prepared to sleep in my van, so I checked into the Hillcrest motel in nearby Luverne, where the people were so kind to me that I stayed there again in later years. They directed me to the Blue Mound Inn for dinner, a place with blue carpet, blue curtains, blue glassware, and dishes with blue patterns.

They served fresh roasted turkey, real mashed potatoes, and something I crave but seldom find—watermelon pickles—a great way to end a great first day on the road!!

Oh I was pleased with myself. I was in a groove, hummin' along feeling the poetry of the road, the collage of light, shining fields, road signs, aromas, the spinning of wheels. I was high.

I felt connected to pure energy. I tuned into Public Radio the next day and heard a blast of Bach organ music just as I crossed into South Dakota with its skies full of huge, rolling cumulus clouds. Seemed the perfect music to accompany this cloud ballet staged against the big blue sky.

I spent the next night in O'Neill, Nebraska, which, according to the guidebook, had the only McDonalds on Rte 20. Never thought of it as a tourist attraction. O'Neill also had a big shamrock painted on the street at the main intersection. I named the motel there the "Crestfallen," the opposite of the Hillcrest where I'd been the night before. It reeked of Lysol and was decorated in a frightening shade of orange.

Working out routes was fun. I tried to find the most interesting or potentially beautiful. I spotted a wild horse sanctuary in Bloomfield, Nebraska. It would be easy to stop there on my way to Valentine, so I did. I parked outside a fence and finally someone arrived who asked if I was there to adopt a horse. Sadly, no, I said, I would just like to watch them. I wanted to become acquainted with the special energy I imagined wild horses would have. Thought I might need it! One horse was outstanding, a tricolor, orange, black and white who was taller than any horse I've ever seen. He had the qualities of a mythical being. I could imagine him as a hero in a fairy tale. What a wild, handsome, spirited tribe they all made. It saddened me to see them confined. But better that than shot dead in the persisting Nevada range wars from where they had been rescued.

Driving away from the wild horse sanctuary, I soon arrived in the land of wild sunflowers, the Sand Hills. I scooted along the northern rim of Nebraska and pulled into Valentine in time for lunch. There was a fairground, grain and feed store, an IGA supermarket, railroad tracks, and a collection of pleasant looking houses but no visible valentines. At a small café, the friendly waitress said I'd find the Snake River and Merritt Lake where it's dammed up if I just went down the road to route 97. Then she added, "Valentine 's so small, you don't need your blinker light, 'cause everyone knows where you're goin' anyway."

I quickly found my route and continued south into rolling ranchland dotted with cattle. The hills that had once been sand dunes in an ancient inland sea, gently rose and fell. Sunlight and cloud shadow tumbled across it, converting that wide, welcoming land into a huge kaleidoscope. A one-room schoolhouse was the only human habitation I passed and there was not a glimpse of the Snake River. Where was it? I was getting a little anxious! About twenty-five miles down the road was a sign, "Snake River Falls Restaurant." A winding dirt road led me to a restaurant that looked a bit like a large cabin. The two young sons of the manager were there. They took me to the beautiful falls a short way behind the building. It's one of only two waterfalls in the entire state of Nebraska.

Had to pay seventy-five cents to see it! But it was more than worth it to see the canyon, its pine filled ridges, the beautiful falls themselves, and to know the Snake River, once the stuff of trance and visions, was really there.

Then these kids offered to take me to their swimming hole a little way up river. I got my swimsuit and "water sox" and they led the way. It was a spot of tender beauty, which I later visited many times. There was a deep pool with little ledges around it. Water trickled and tinkled in little falls between mosses and wildflowers. A cloud of blue dragonflies hovered above. Red pines stood on the banks and cattle lowed nearby. I saw the purplish cone-shaped nests of mud swallows. I had seen them in trance but had no idea what they were at the time. I felt at home. I relaxed into a state of wonder.

Leaving those boys and their goofy chocolate lab pup named Magnum Blatt, their family name, I continued down the road to Merritt Lake where there was a trading post and some cabins. Jon, the owner, said he and his family were "Sand Hill converts" from Pennsylvania. I rented one of their cabins. They were happy to tell me the places where I could approach the Snake River. They also told me about the wildlife refuges nearby. Their enthusiasm and generous sharing of information was so reassuring I felt it was perfectly natural for me to be there. When anyone asked why I had come, I said that I was an artist and that answer always seemed sufficient. Any tentative feelings I had about this journey dissipated.

Pelicans And The Hunting/Fishing Club

The memory of the meditation cave I'd seen in trance was pressing and that meant exploring the river wherever it was possible to get near it. Would I find the place I had "seen?" I wanted to be in my "cave" for the full moon in July. I knew from Joe the old White Buffalo Calf Pipe of the Sioux would be brought out for a ceremony that night in Green Grass. I was feeling indefinable connections with Green Grass here. Feelings of connection, like filaments of light, were an invisible map that often guided me. I learned to trust those feelings.

I walked for hours on the beaches surrounding the lake. It was a paradise for birds. I was amazed to see flocks of majestic white pelicans coasting in. Hawks circled, red-headed woodpeckers knocked on the cottonwoods, goldfinches sprang up everywhere, enormous blue herons stalked the rims of the lake, and wild turkeys chortled from the bush and meadowlarks were everywhere.

The refuges were vast marshes seemingly owned by redwing blackbirds riding the tall grasses. One very hot day, what Jon called "a cooker," when I wandered into a refuge from the road I was mobbed by curlews and assaulted by their persistent high-pitched cries. Suddenly I lost my sense of direction, unable to think of any landmark I had passed. I realized how absolutely alone I was in this implacable vastness. Menacing black clouds rose from the horizon. Thunder rumbled in the distance. I held my breath. I felt I was drifting, shedding my body! I kept thinking of the dead. In spite of the heat I was in a cold sweat, shaking from head to foot! After some deep breathing and clutching a sweet feather I discovered at my feet, I regained my stability, and trembling, found my way back to the van. Never saw anything so lovely as that van! Only then did I remember reading that the Sioux called the Sand Hills, "the land of the gone before ones, not a place to go before the Death Song." And when people did venture there, "if they came back, the tongue was twisted and none could understand." Black Elk had said it was "the home of the ancestors." I felt like I'd had a narrow escape!

At the time I was deep into *Old Jules*, the book written by Mari Sandoz about growing up in Nebraska's Sand Hills and its staggering hardships. It became clear to me what a miraculous oasis the Snake was and is, a green cleft abundant with life, in the immensity of that sandy land.

The cabins at the trading post were really for fishermen. I enjoyed staying there but on the day I saw one of my neighbors dispatch his living catch with an electric steak knife, I decided to join the Snake River Hunting and Fishing Club and stay in one of its five cabins next to the restaurant and falls. It was $250 a year and $15 a night for the privilege of staying in heaven. I already knew I'd return the next year if the Club accepted me.

First, I had to speak with the president of the Club, a lawyer from Lincoln, and that went fine. I said I wouldn't be hunting or fishing, just drawing and writing. Bill Blatt, the manager, said he'd be glad for some company on the river, as there was seldom anyone there.

My cabin was on the edge of the Snake River canyon, with pines all around. It had two rooms, a little kitchen and bath. The furniture was old and comfy. I returned the twenty-five miles to Valentine and loaded up with supplies and settled in. Carol had warned me that green veggies were few and far between in this part of the world and the only available lettuce was iceberg. Indeed, a BLT became my idea of a balanced meal. I imagined getting scurvy in Nebraska. Carol reported that one time at a café there, she gulped down some parsley that was on top of her eggs and the horrified waitress exclaimed, "Well now, hon, If I'd a known you was gonna eat that thing, I woulda warshed it!" I thought of Carol the many times I devoured a little sprig of parsley!

Robin Is My Guide

I learned to relax there by the Snake, to allow each day to suggest itself unburdened by plans and expectations, except of course my quest to find that little cave. I spent five and six hours a day hiking the river and drinking in its diversity, the songs of birds, wind, and cascading waters. I sketched rocks, root systems, pine and cedar trees, and all the wildflowers. I especially loved the white poppies. In doing a study of a pinecone I felt I was seeing the structure of the "tree of life." Clement Greenberg used to say that we are "made helpless" before great art. I think we are also made helpless before the wonders of the earth and that is why we do not "see" it and even do terrible things to avoid acknowledging it. We have turned great art into dollar signs and the wonderful earth into real estate to protect ourselves from the helpless state of awe and wonder.

I packed picnic lunches and simply lived in my bathing suit and water sox. I believed I was becoming reacquainted with the world of my former life. Sometimes it seemed the river itself was instructing me. I heard things like:

"... those plants found in river islands receive the greatest strength from both river and earth" and, "the river delights in its being ... it is not always thinking of its work and purposes" and, "along its path it is fed by springs from the earth which refresh it and add to its vigor." According to my journal from that time, I was "scratched, bit, bruised, bumped, bashed, and rashed but happy" from hiking the twists and turns of that dear river.

Evenings I'd drive to the lake to see the sunset or take that goofy lab, Magnum, for a run. Magnum's presence reminded me that I had seen a wolf-like dog as my companion in that previous lifetime on the Snake. While Magnum was far from being wolfish, he was a great friend.

A robin perched on my picnic table one morning. It seemed to say it would be my guide for the day. I decided to follow it. It led me deeper into the canyon, always staying just above me. I climbed up and down keeping an eye on the river below and the robin above, and didn't see a group of deer on the bank until the large doe pawed the earth and barked at me. Do deer bark? Yes, they do, and they can be very aggressive. Frightened, I made myself as small as possible. They glared at me but finally decided to retreat.

My robin flew off but not before leading me to view a nest of red-tailed hawks and the cave-like place high up in the canyon that fit what I'd seen in trance as the spot for my full moon meditation. I later thanked that robin by writing a song about it called, "Robin Adventure Bird." A part of the lyric is, "I want to go where you go, see what you see, know what you know, Robin." It's on an album I recorded to celebrate the arrival of my first granddaughter and I still think those words whenever I see a robin.

I discovered a way to reach that little cave-like hollow from the rim of the canyon and was content that it was "the" place. The night of the full moon was only a couple of days away. I announced my plans to spend that night on the river. Everyone said "Well, what about snakes, coyotes, and skunks?" (Just a few of the things that were mentioned.) I gave them a ho-hum look and proceeded with my plans. I called Joan in New York for a little encouragement. She said the medicine teacher from my former life there might make an appearance. I definitely did not mention this to Bill or the people at the trading post! On the 19th of July, I rolled up a mat and popped it into my backpack along with sage and tobacco for prayers and Snicker bars, my preferred breakfast at the time. After supper I made my way along the canyon rim and dropped down onto a ledge and settled into the hollow. A nest of squeaking baby swallows welcomed me. There were some tracks and scat but they looked old.

The coming of night was announced by dancing fireflies. When darkness closed in around 10 o'clock, I could see the light of the rising moon reflected on the opposite side of the canyon. The canyon seemed a very different place in moonlight. It was barely recognizable as the canyon I knew from daytime hikes. I felt uneasy. Stars emerged and again I saw threads of light connecting them and was thrilled. Among the many prayers I offered that night was one for the magnificent wild horse I had seen at the sanctuary in Bloomfield. As I prayed for him to get a good home, a brilliant shooting star flew down right in front of me. Bingo, that prayer was answered!

Later on, looking down at the river I saw a spot where light was accumulating.

I watched it grow into a shimmering blue column. It rose from the water and stood trembling there for a time and then disappeared. Was it a river spirit, a spirit of the earth, a manifestation of my former teacher? Whatever it was, it was magical and beautiful and I felt so blessed. Most of all I felt deeply grateful that I was alive when so many I knew were dying or already gone. Not only was I alive, but in a sense, simultaneously re-living an earlier lifetime. So, I was doubly alive!

In every way life on the Snake was very different from NYC. Planes landed and took off on the road, mail was picked up three times a week at a mailbox a couple of miles away, and I often got caught in the middle of cattle drives, a very different kind of traffic jam! I was aware every day of the direction and velocity of the wind because there was nothing to stop it. I was always conscious of nature, unlike NYC where we are so insulated.

The weather service predicted a 30% chance of rain every day but it seldom occurred. When storms descended they were awe-inspiring displays of yellow, orange, purple, and blue lightning. I had a front row seat at the show when winds flew from every direction, rain in huge drops turned to ether, the sky becoming red was momentarily streaked by black lightning, and wind sang in a sobbing minor key into the deafening percussion of thunder. I imagined I was on a journey in the wild cosmos.

Green Grass And The Tree Of Life

The date of the Sundance was approaching. I was determined to support Joe even though I was deeply absorbed by happy days as a member of the Snake River Hunting and Fishing Club. I pulled out a map of South Dakota. The location of the Sundance was nowhere to be found but I knew Green Grass was somewhere near Eagle Butte and that, at least, appeared on the map. It was in the Cheyenne River Reservation. I quickly decided not to use that ugly word, "reservation" and instead, referred to "The Cheyenne River Branch of the Sioux Nation." I drove north from Valentine up through the Rosebud Reservation, simply known as" The Rosebud." It was my first venture into Indian territory and I was anxious, about what, I'm not sure, maybe some cultural detritus floating about in my psyche.

It was the vastness of prairie and sky that was most intimidating. I felt adrift in all that space and hunkered down behind the wheel of the van feeling that huge sky might swallow me whole. In comparison, the Sand Hills felt almost cozy!

Eagle Butte had a steak house, a coffee shop, a cultural center, and a small motel whose owner was a scowling white woman who made you feel that you were probably a criminal, but I stayed there one night and then ventured out in search of Green Grass. There were no signs and directions were sketchy and nothing was green. But I found it, a small collection of government houses perched on a hill above the Little Moreau River where old cottonwoods provided the only green visible for miles. Further down the rutted dirt road from the houses were a few trailers where the Looking Horse family lived. The Looking Horse family has been the keeper of the old White Buffalo Calf Pipe for nineteen generations. Perhaps this was the very place that the White Buffalo Calf Woman appeared when she came to teach people about the Pipe. Arvol Looking Horse, the family member in charge, had a vision around the time of the Harmonic Convergence that led him to sponsor this Sundance, which was the first of four to be given over a period of four years.

Joe saw me pull in. He explained in his solemn way the ceremony would be on the other side of the river, that I must drive across it, camp over there, and meantime pick sage for the lodge of the dancers and remember to give tobacco as thanks to the sage. I was not to pick the tall ones, which are the grandparent plants, or the female sage full of seeds, or the buffalo sage because it makes the skin itch. Sure, Joe, yeah! Wow, was I out of my depth! It was a world unimaginable in New York City.

But then, drumming began. The resounding beat of the great Lakota drum thrust me back in time and into a different consciousness. A wave of great peace and joy swept over me. I belonged here. The drum is more than a meter in diameter and usually played by a group of men. Its deep vibration is a sound that can be heard and felt for great distances, even the distance of an earlier lifetime. I quickly bent to the task of picking and giving thanks to the sage and as I did so, spotted the inquisitive face of a puma peeking through the dry brown grasses before quickly disappearing. The rattlesnakes had already been carried out of the area, not killed.

I held my breath and drove across the river with people laughing and cheering me on. In following years kids would run to ride with me, waiting to hear the power yell I gave to exhort the latest "Vanita von Van" across the river and up the opposite muddy bank, where I would wait to hear their excited shrieks of laughter! Sometimes I sang, "Vanita von Van, she does what she can, she who eats road like pie a la mode!"

Once across, I parked beneath a gracious cottonwood with some of Joe's friends, who were artists from St Paul. We were the only non-natives present. We were a curiosity so we had an almost continuous flow of visitors and the coffee pot never left the fire. Coffee native style is simply tossed in the pot with water and boiled with an egg to take out the bitterness. It was later said that a spoon could stand straight up in a cup of coffee prepared by me. Nice to be known for something!

I looked out at the lay of the land. It was a wide circle and the circular Sundance ring had an arbor, which was later roofed with leafy cottonwood branches. It was built near the foot of a protective hill. Circling the hills were men riding horses. They rode on blankets, not saddles. With heads held high they patrolled the hilltops. There was a sense that we were close to enemy territory. Native people often experienced hostilities. The American Indian Religious Freedom Act (AIRFA) had been passed only eleven years before in 1978. Statistically speaking, one in ten Native Americans has been a victim of hate crimes, with many more unreported. The riders of Green Grass wanted to be sure the ceremony, the dancers, and all of us, were safe.

It was nearly dusk when people suddenly ran to their cars. I jumped into my van and followed. I forgot I'd stashed my box of paints beneath it. They were a bit bruised but not, thankfully, destroyed!

The procession bounced along the land until reaching a young cottonwood standing alone in a clearing. This was the tree the medicine man had chosen to be in the center of the Sundance ring. A red ribbon was tied around it. Two little girls came forward. Vincent Black Feather, the medicine man, bent to speak with them, then handed them an axe. Each girl tapped the tree with the axe. Then it was cut it down but not allowed to fall. It was carried tenderly to the back of a truck and driven off to the Sundance ring. There, it was laid on the quilts of the dancers and their supporters. I didn't have a quilt so I added my nice sunflower towel. While the tree rested on this collage of quilts and one towel, prayer flags were tied to it. It was considered a blessing if the tree left a leaf on your quilt and I did receive one. It was a very solemn moment. The sacrifice of this tree standing for the legendary "Tree of Life," was the beginning of the Sundance, a ceremony of sacrifice. For four years I cried when the Sundance tree was cut down.

Sleeping in my van for the first time that night I felt cozy and safe. I listened to the clacking of the leathery cottonwood leaves, the neighing of horses and the swish-swish of their tails. I could see stars through my window. I was deeply happy.

I learned how to gather twigs to make a campfire, and cook over it, activities very foreign to a New York apartment dweller. I learned to use water with care, saving some to cook and some to wash. It all had to be carried in and we were asked to use it respectfully as the dancers would not be drinking water for four days. Then, importantly, I learned to run to the outhouse before sunrise because that's when the flies wake up! Outwitting flies was a constant during Sundances, to say nothing of dodging armies of grasshoppers.

A Buffalo Dancer And Eagle Whistles

The ceremony began at dawn when the Buffalo Dancer entered the ring through the opening in the east. His name was Rufus. He carried a buffalo hide staff and wore a buffalo headdress. His step, his body, and head swayed as a buffalo while he slowly danced around the ring. His long skirt was in the sacred color of red, his torso was painted in a yellow design, and there were white marks under his eyes. He had two long gray braids. He made us believe he was the buffalo come to bless the dance. He was a solemn man who emitted great strength and benevolence.

The dancers, led by medicine man Vincent Black Feather, entered the Sundance ring and the drums and singing began.

The dancers wore long skirts in different colors. Some had images of their individual totems sewn on the cloth. Joe wore purple. Their heads were crowned with sage circlets and they wore sage bracelets and anklets. They blew their eagle bone whistles and were sometimes answered by the shrill cries of an eagle above. They danced slowly in place gazing up at the sun. The tree began to glow with a visible aura. It seemed to pull us toward it. On this day and the next the Pipes of the dancers were brought to us, their supporters. We were invited to smoke them while we danced in the shaded arbor.

The sound of the eagle whistles, the deep vibration of the drum, the relentless sun, the wailing singers, all wore away any sense I had of myself and filled me with the ancient recognition of how utterly vulnerable humanity on its small planet is. I knew these people danced, prayed, and sacrificed for all of us.

I wore a large shawl, as all the women did, and I cried most of the time. I cried for these people, the earth, my friends who were dying, and I cried for myself. I asked each tear to be a prayer.

On the third day of this Sundance, the chests of the men were pierced by the Medicine man using a surgical blade and an alcohol wipe for this purpose. It was the Indian Health

Service that made this requirement because AIDS was spreading among Indian peoples as it was everywhere, offering a painful reminder of the burden of grief I already carried. The skin over the dancers' pectorals was greased with bear fat before pegs were inserted in through the skin. Long ropes attached the pegs to the Sundance Tree.

The ropes had been attached to the tree from the first day of the dance to remind the men of the sacrifice they would make. They danced and pulled, touching the tree repeatedly for strength until the pegs were torn from their flesh. Many experienced trance. Some were quickly released, others had a very hard time. The few women sundancers, (who were not attached to the tree), gave small flesh offerings from their arms. The dancers said the only thing you can really own and sacrifice is your own flesh. I fervently hoped the prayers of the dancers were answered.

On the second day of the ceremony Joe left the lodge where the dancers rested and slept. He was very disturbed. He believed his special hawk claw, a symbol of his protective totem, had disappeared. When it was soon recovered, Joe wanted to reenter the ceremony, but the medicine man told him he must wait two years before trying again. Thankfully, Joe's lovely companion, Sara, was present to bring comfort and wisdom to him. All of us in Joe's camp were sad for him but thanked him for trying and for bringing all of us together for this deeply inspiring time. We urged him to rest among us for the remaining days of the ceremony.

While later dancing in the arbor on that distressing day, I saw distinct animal forms in the passing clouds. My journal from that time lists: frog, bear, eagle, and spider.

Suddenly I remembered my book of animal silhouettes in the van. I shared it and a photo of the Vieques altar with the camp. Someone said, "Without a boulder, why not paint them on individual stones?" Of course, obvious, too obvious for me to think of it! Joe's friends scoured the hills and found enough rocks with paintable surfaces for me to complete a circle of 22 stones. Some of those stones, with beautiful fossils from the time of the ancient inland sea, I put aside.

I worked hard, painting in dry heat, amid clouds of grasshoppers while being bitten by flies and I had dust between my teeth from the strong winds! It took grit! I painted during the dancers' rest periods whenever possible and enjoyed the company of curious children and others who wanted to know what I was doing. It was the first rock circle of nearly sixty that I have painted around the world. There was one really nosey visitor to our camp, a woman named Carmelita. We discovered she was sent by the organizers of the Sundance to make sure no women in our group of outsiders were "on their moon," i.e. menstruating, which is believed to create danger to the ceremony. There was a tipi on the other side of the river for these women.

At the conclusion of the four-day dance, those amazing dancers, both men and women, stood in line and we were able to shake their hands. At the beginning of the line I found a plant I had seen in a vision that called itself "fingers of the earth." I put my hands into it. It seemed to fill my hands with tremendous positive energy because I, a stranger, was repeatedly embraced and my hands clung to.

Then we headed into Eagle Butte to take much-needed showers available at the school gymnasium. It didn't matter the water was icy cold and only dribbled. I claimed the water running off our bodies looked like a mudslide. At the conclusion of the Sundance there was a feast provided by two deer and an antelope. It all seemed familiar and natural for the 19th century where it felt I had been transported.

Before leaving I touched the Sundance tree, took a small piece of bark and little bit of earth from the ground to use in blessing my home on the Snake River of Nebraska.

A Stone Circle

I wanted the stone circle I had been painting to stay in Green Grass and had to ask permission from Arvol Looking Horse to leave it there. He was such an imposing figure, I felt intimidated by him. Joe's friend Sara went with me to speak to Arvol. We held hands for courage. Joe actually laughed at the two of us and reminded us we must give the traditional gift of tobacco that precedes any conversation with a chief or medicine person. When we gave Arvol the tobacco, he simply nodded, but when I showed him some stones and said it had been "given to me" to paint them he looked again, then gestured to a spot across from the octagonal wooden Pipe House where the ancient Buffalo Calf Pipe is kept.

Sara, some children and a local woman helped me carry them. As I walked up the hill with the eagle stone, an eagle appeared and circled above me honoring the work! I placed a pinch of tobacco in thanks beneath each stone. Before I left, Arvol came to me with tears in his eyes and simply said, "Thank you for..." paused but couldn't say any more. I told him I hoped to return the next year. He seemed doubtful and said, "It was only a dream." I replied dreams are the greatest teachers and then he smiled. It was so good to see a smile on that gaunt and dour face.

At the remaining Sundances over the next three years, I painted additional circles for the same place. This was perhaps the most joyous work of my life! I was re-experiencing a past life I had truly loved in the beautiful present and was filled with wonder and hope for the future of our beloved Earth. I knew this ceremony was powerful way beyond my understanding.

Painting this first circle inspired me. I began to imagine that my response to the starry web of light I had seen would be a web of stone circles. I imagined Bear Butte as the center of the web, and that I could connect the painted stone circles energetically to the mountain by burying a small stone from the mountain in the center of each circle. I did, in fact, place a stone from Bear Butte wrapped in sage at the center of this first circle. I imagined threads of light running from Bear Butte to the circles and between the circles themselves, creating an earthbound artist's "hello" to the starry heavens. And I decided that my signature for the circles would be a gold spider web on a waving blade of green grass, honoring two sacred places, Bear Butte and Green Grass, home of the ancient Pipe.

At the time of that first Sundance, Arvol Looking Horse had never left South Dakota and could scarcely converse in English. But he was rapidly transformed into a great and articulate leader, even traveling to Iraq with the hope of sharing his Pipe with Saddam Hussein in an effort to bring peace on the eve of the first of those wars. He gave a speech in New York at that time and on later occasions. He started the Big Foot ride, a reenactment of the journey of Chief Big Foot in icy December weather to Wounded Knee where his band was massacred. After several years of this reenactment the local people greeted Arvol and the riders with warm food and drink, and so the process of healing began.

I wonder what Arvol was experiencing during these Sundances. He is a courageous man of profound faith, a real hero.

Among the visitors to Joe's camp during the Sundance were Robert Grey Bear and his sister Mona, both from Eagle Butte. In fact, they often stopped by for a cup of my notorious coffee. They were more outgoing than most of the residents of Green Grass and Eagle Butte. Robert had attended Berkeley for two years until the chief, Stanley Looking Horse, warned him against "white man's ways." Mona went to college for a time where she reigned as a beauty queen. They were both friendly and light-hearted and I was so glad they were eager for me to return because, much to my surprise, that was my clear intention in spite of my complex life in NYC. The land, the people, the ceremony, the drums, all were suddenly and firmly me. It felt a bit like love at first sight while a part of me was simultaneously sensing how much I had once loved my previous life as a native on the Great Plains.

Robert Grey Bear invited me to give some art classes the following year at the H.V. Johnston Sioux Cultural Center in Eagle Butte. He was curator there. I could hardly wait! But it was time to leave Green Grass and Eagle Butte and return to the Sand Hills of Nebraska. On the way out of town I stopped at a car wash. "Vanita von Van" was unkempt to say the least! The guy at the car wash said, "Well, now ma'am, you sure you need a wash? Cause I can still tell the color of this here van." He had a great smile and I was glad to laugh.

Sand Hill Adventures

*I*t was hard to drive away from that special world. I could still hear and feel the vibrations of the drums and the Sundance songs long after I left. Lucky for me I had that little cabin on the Snake to look forward to, a quiet place where I could process all the sensations and thoughts aroused by the Sundance.

I loved that cabin, even on the night the bathroom ceiling caved in from the weight of years of mouse droppings. Squeaking chaos and wild confusion! I laughed until I cried and until all the mice found their way out. I already had regular mouse visitors, one named, "mouse klutz" because it knocked over whatever was in its path, the other, "supermouse" who seemed to fly.

Sometimes I had supper at the little restaurant with its décor of animal skins and heads. I think I alarmed Bill by delivering a caustic scientific lecture about an imagined planet where animals prevailed and human heads were on the wall. I wasn't entirely kidding when I threatened to remove the coyote skin on the restaurant's wall and give it a decent burial. One Friday evening when I dropped in for a hamburger, three young men marched in, clean-shaven, boots polished, shirts crisp, and jeans pressed. One of them paused next to my table. If I'd given the slightest sign of interest, I think I would have been lassoed and carried off. Bill hurried to my table and quietly explained these men were from remote ranches in search of wives. They didn't have the opportunity or time to find or court women and were on the hunt. There was an air of desperation about them. I retreated to my cabin, locked the door, and wondered about the lives they led.

Then there was the morning that Bill pounded on my cabin door before dawn, shouting he needed help in the kitchen. A group of firefighters was arriving after a long night of beating back a prairie fire started by ball lightning. I'd never heard of such a thing and tried to imagine it skipping over the hills. Minutes later I was wearing an apron and saying, "fried or scrambled" to a group of exhausted young people from the Job Corps. This was my one and only experience as a waitress and to me it was fun, even a bit exotic.

And I learned that if a prairie fire headed toward the Snake, I must go down to the river and climb up to the ledge behind the falls. I tried it later. I wanted to know if I could do it. It was a bit like walking to the Nuyorican Poets Cafe on Third Street, NYC at night, past the Hell's Angels headquarters—breathless with the happy feeling of winning a childhood dare! "I did it, I did it!"

I drove as many roads around the Sand Hills as I could find. Very few were paved and all, seldom traveled. There were no towns, stores or resorts. I seldom saw another vehicle. This stark, undulating land seemed immeasurably beautiful to me. It filled me with a mysterious nostalgia. I couldn't get enough of it.

There wasn't much road-kill on these back roads but enough to awaken both fury and sadness in my heart. Beautiful creatures dead in the road left to be hit again and again. I got in the habit of picking them up when I wouldn't be in danger of becoming road-kill myself. It was Joe Geshick who awakened me to the sacredness of all life when he became distressed at the sight of a dead beaver flung on the ground next to a public path. Why, he asked, had no one buried it or given an offering to thank it for its time on earth? He was angry that no respect had been expressed, and I felt the same way. Whenever possible I removed them from the road, put them safely on the earth, and gave a prayer. One Christmas my daughters presented me with a very lovely hand woven pouch full of plastic gloves for my "road kill ministry." They were concerned I would "pick up something" from these poor creatures.

In the Sand Hills I once scooped a road-killed hawk from the road, tied ribbons to its feet and carried it out into the hills. As I gave tobacco to its spirit and sang to it, a pick-up rumbled up. It was a park ranger who was visiting the so-called National Forest nearby. I say, "so-called" because it was a handful of trees on vast tracks of grazing land. I had naively imagined that National Forest was really forest, not ranch land and tree farms, which is what it seems to be more often than not.

This ranger was just curious about the lone figure on the horizon – me, of all people! There were times when I scarcely believed myself. Was I really an artist from NYC, a place where cement is always underfoot and the heavens are hidden by skyscrapers?

The ranger was a Mormon from Utah. He liked my send-off for this splendid bird and told me it was a Swainson's hawk. He was studying the diet of porcupines and later sent me his findings, which made for odd reading in New York City! You never know what will be helpful because in Bali, Indonesia a few years later, I had pet porcupines and I knew how to take care of them. I met Dave, the ranger, again in Idaho and he took me along a track that grizzlies had made from Montana into Yellowstone. I saw the crushed wildflowers where a grizzly had been sleeping. I picked some and hoped the grizzly was well on its way. I still have those old dried pressed flowers full of grizzly bear dreams. Dave said the park service was trying to determine if the construction of a new road would interfere with the grizzly migrations. There is an invisible map of animal trails all over the continent and I am always so happy to discover a bit of it. It's reassuring to know that a part of the planet is still shared. The people in Dave's office knew about the ceremony I had for the hawk and pointed, "Oh, you're the one who...," and studied me quizzically.

That hawk was the first road-kill I picked up. In New York City we don't have road-kill unless you count the occasional flattened pigeon.

It was a snake on the road to Valentine that I picked up next. My friend Christina, whom I'd met on the wolf-tracking project, was visiting me. She said a snakeskin would be helpful in the nature classes she taught in Brooklyn. How to skin it? A woman from Manhattan and a woman from Brooklyn didn't know much about skinning snakes! We joked about the male snakes we'd like to skin. In fact, the women of her tribe, the Cherokee, used to do just that, but long ago. The Game Warden of Cherry County happened to stop by "the Club" and Bill told him he had some guests who needed his help. The warden taught us how to skin it: "Cut off the head, then peel back the skin like you pull down your socks. Nothin' to it." We did it. Well, New Yorkers can do anything. I took the head, wrapped it in sage and tobacco and red cloth and hung it from a tree above the river. We put the snake meat on a bed of sage and carried it out into the hills. The minute we put it down, the sun broke through a cloudy sky and an eagle hovered above looking down on the good meal awaiting it. The kids in Christina's Brooklyn classes were impressed with their teacher and the beautiful snakeskin she displayed.

That Game Warden helped out again. On the way to Valentine one morning for a haircut, I moved a dead porcupine off the road. I mentioned the porcupine to Twylla, the haircutter, who was a Lakota from "The Rosebud." She told me a lot of women on the Rosebud did quill work and always needed quills. It's a beautiful and elaborate art! "Maybe," she said, "if you see any more porcupines, you could bring 'em to me and I'll take 'em up to the rez." When I told the Warden about this he surprised me by being genuinely pleased. "Terrible waste." he said. He offered to deliver to Twylla any porcupines that either of us picked up. The sole of a porcupine's foot is one of the most tender, vulnerable things I have ever seen. I hated to see them hit but was glad for the "Porcupine Express" to the Rosebud. I declared then, that if ever I became rich, I would build a monument to the animals killed on the road. I liked to visualize that towering monument standing in the Mall in DC!

In New York City I would never have imagined speaking to a game warden, picking up road kill, and much else that was too foreign for conversation there. Eventually I was able to share my experiences through story telling performances as a way of communicating my adventures. The first one, about the Sand Hills and South Dakota was called "Roadshow." Some lines from a poem I wrote for that performance playfully warned the New York audience to prepare for adventures in a land hitherto unknown to them or to me, the driver/ storyteller.

> Road alert
> Red alert
> Road conditions end
> Dirt ruts
> Dust tracks
> Fade into the wind
> Steady now
> Breathe deep
> Here a path begins.

Although we were no longer living together, my dear Eric was in the audience, and laughed so much at some of the episodes I described, he claimed he felt much better than he had for quite a time.

It was Eric who first introduced me to the Sand Hills and it was the last place that I saw him. As his health failed, he moved back to his family home in Omaha. He wanted to die at home. Frail and feverish, he drove up to see me on the Snake. In Valentine the Cherry County Fair was in full swing and a circle of my painted rocks was on display. I had met a group of women artists, "The Sand Hill Painters," and they invited me to join their show at the Fair. Their kindness meant a lot to me. How Eric laughed to see me, his *Uptown Girl,* so at home in the far reaches of Nebraska, and participating in the County Fair no less!

I chipped a front tooth while he was there. In the dentist's office, Eric held my hand with such tenderness that all the love we had felt for one another, all that we had shared, suddenly flowered and flowed through us and shone before us in a mere breath of time that was both wonderful and devastating.

How absurd it seemed that the setting for such a moment, the stuff of grand opera, should be in a dentist's office.

That year, 1992, the long drought in the Midwest was really over and the Sand Hills looked like pale green velvet. I drove Eric to my favorite places, saving the best for last, the hills blanketed with wild sunflowers swaying in the sunlight. For a long time we sat and watched the dancing of light and shadow over those golden blossoms, their faces eagerly turned to the sun. We made a pact then, to find each other in the next lifetime with "sunflower," as our password. When Eric left I watched him drive away in the black pick-up he called "Angus." I watched until I couldn't see him anymore. I knew I'd never see him again. It was hard to breathe. I didn't know what to do with myself. I looked down, saw some sage, put my hands in it, tried to pick some but none would come. I followed a line of it, touching it, bending to breathe it in, still trying to pick it until it brought me to a beautiful hawk feather, the gift that tells you to lift your gaze and circle the wide horizons. I held that feather against my heart and sobbed until I couldn't anymore.

Coyote And Crazy Horse

A local brochure about the Sand Hills reported that Caroline Sandoz lived nearby. She was the youngest sister of Mari Sandoz, who wrote *Cheyenne Autumn, Old Jules,* the story of her father, and a biography of *Crazy Horse, Strange Man of the Ogallalas.* Jules was a pioneer who lived in a sod house with his family. They endured the excruciating hardships of prairie wind, snow and hunger.

I called Caroline. She said she'd be in, so I set off to find her. I learned in our conversation that the spring that was the source of the Snake River, was on her land. I'm not sure what I imagined it would look like, but felt surprised when I saw it was just another marsh, a small one.

Caroline's home was quite a long way off the main road on which I had seen only a coyote, a hawk, a deer, and a truck. That coyote stopped and stared right at me and later I was compelled to paint a picture of it. Caroline said she was surprised I'd seen so much!

The empty roads were, for me, one of the appeals of the area. I could dawdle, stop and stare without someone shaking a fist at me, or worse! Near Caroline's house was the orchard, which Jules, long ago, had forced his family to plant. It's a bit of a legend in the treeless Sand Hills.

When Caroline opened the door, she looked at me as though I'd just dropped in from Mars, and I didn't blame her because I kind of felt that way myself. But then she was very gracious. The memorabilia of Mari and the family were in the basement. It was a cross between a museum and a shrine. Caroline was like a medium connecting me to the 19th century. I asked if it was true that Mari had commissioned a portrait of Crazy Horse from a compilation of descriptions given by Sioux elders. Caroline smiled and went to a drawer and pulled out a small photograph of the portrait. She looked at me for a moment and then said, "Please, I want you to have this." I told her I had loved Crazy Horse ever since I'd read her sister's book about him and that her gift was a great treasure. I showed her a photo of one of my paintings and she said it was like Diego Rivera, whom she admired.

She didn't know about the work of his wife, Frida Kahlo, so I had fun telling her about it.

She expressed concern over the possibility of selling water from the great Nebraska aquifer. She said she was part of a group protesting that. She was also planting trees for migrating birds. A great lady she was! I was sad to leave and I think the feeling was mutual. If I couldn't find a place to stay in Gordon, my destination, she invited me to return and stay with her. Wish I had, but I was hoping to find a young Native American couple I knew in New York who had decided to manage a motel in that tough cow town at the edge of the Pine Ridge Reservation. When I got to the motel, the manager, an older woman told me they had given up. She was a strong, determined lady who crocheted. I bought some of her beautiful work and spent the night.

Crazy Horse was a visionary, a loner, a great warrior and lover. Who needs knights in shining armor? I drove to as many of his old haunts as I could find in that part of Nebraska and South Dakota. I tried to imagine him and his band on their ponies, hiding from the blue coats. I also went to Fort Robinson where he was betrayed and murdered. I plucked a small branch from an old cottonwood tree there and carried it with me for a long time.

I ventured into the Badlands on these jaunts, privately calling them the Goodlands. Their stark colorful beauty, their ancientness and silence are profound. Joanie, who frequents the Badlands, had told me about Sheep Table Mountain and said I should visit it. I gathered the courage before dawn one morning to drive the lonely, dusty, deeply rutted roads that wound upward to the top of the Table. The view was breathtaking and the rainbow palette of the sandstone formations burst into life in the first gold rays of the rising sun.

When I opened the van door there was roar. I had startled a large flock of rock doves, i.e., pigeons, and the rush of their wings as they flew up from a ledge was like the sound of a chainsaw in the deep silence of the Badlands. You can scarcely hear a wing flap in New York City. There, you would never imagine it possible to be scared by a flock of pigeons! I heard a coyote and howled back to it. Soon a group of coyotes was replying and seemed to be getting closer but I lost my nerve and took off. The following year I took a friend up there, praising the beauty and rareness and silence of the place. When we reached the top of the Table we were greeted by movie cowboys, big trailers, and techs running around with bullhorns; then a helicopter appeared. It was a Marlboro shoot! I've always thought of this as "Coyote's Revenge" Did I really think I could fool Coyote, that legendary trickster, and get away with it?

I sometimes stopped at a café near the Badlands. The owner was a woman who cared about the local people and tried to help out. She pointed out a painted skull on one of my visits. The artist, she said, was a young Lakota man whom she felt had a good future. We talked about the problems of being an artist, and being an Indian, probably insurmountable. I left my address and a small contribution for the artist. When I returned to New York, there was a letter waiting for me from this young man and enclosed was an eagle feather! My second eagle feather, and a real beauty. It hangs now from the Pipe I was later given. It arrived just in time. The eagle feather from Joe had just been devoured by that grasshopper trapped in my van during a Sundance.

The young artist, whose name was Scott Lupi, invited me to visit him in his home on the "The Pine Ridge," the reservation which is the site of Wounded Knee. He lived in Kyle, near Wanblee. Wanblee had been the home of Crazy Horse. People told me his relatives are still there. The next year when I was in the Badlands again, I drove into Wanblee, which means, "eagle" in the Lakota language, and indeed an eagle flew across the hood of my van, skimming it. The appearance of an eagle is always an auspicious sign and thrilling occurrence. It certainly impressed an old Indian couple I had picked up. They were drunk and wanted a ride to the nearest town where alcohol was sold. They were babbling, trying to talk me out of some money until that eagle appeared and then they were quiet and respectful.

People on foot are not unusual on these lonely roads. They are sometimes inebriated and searching for another drink. In the winter they often die in snowdrifts. That is what happened to the granddaughter of a woman who befriended me in Green Grass. Alcoholism is a tragedy that creates chains of tragedies on the reservation. Volumes could be written about it. I was always aware of how blessed I was in the Native American people I met, people who survived, and triumphed in the most terrible environments and went on to unselfishly inspire others, including myself. When I got to Kyle and found Scott's house, he came right out to greet me though I hadn't been able to tell him what day or week I would arrive. He "just knew." I had painted a rock with a horse and stars for Scott. He had painted a stone for me with a horse on one side and the Pleiades on the other. We stood and laughed with real joy at these unexpected and so perfect gifts. He said he tried not to speak the name of Crazy Horse too often for fear of disturbing that great hero's journey in the afterlife. And he added, "You're the second prayer person I've met out here." Well now, hmm, did I miss something? Is that what I am! Scott said the other "prayer person" was a woman in the Black Hills who played music for the forest. I said I hoped I would meet her.

Rock Circles And A Bear Guide

*I*loved being on the road, the freedom and adventure of it, the unfolding of the wonders of the earth day by day. My cabin on the Snake River was the perfect jumping off place and the perfect place to return to after visits to Bear Butte, the Sundances in Green Grass and journeys across the country painting stone circles. It felt like home.

I felt attuned to the migrating species of the continent and liked to imagine they shared the exuberance I felt on my journeys. Although I felt timid when confronting wide-open spaces and unfamiliar terrain, my zest for them rapidly grew. So many people I met imagined that I was courageous to live in New York City, a place where I was entirely at ease. It's a grid. There's Uptown and Downtown, the West side and the East side and most streets are numbered. It's nothing like trying to find your way in the sky, which is how it often felt out on the Great Plains. Out there, people thought nothing of driving 100 miles for dinner. In New York sometimes just crossing town for dinner was a big deal.

In the Midwest and elsewhere, New York was seen as a violent and dangerous place because, as usual, the media focused on crime. People sometimes regarded me with suspicion as though I were a foreign and possibly dangerous species. When this occurred, I lowered my energy to a, "I Couldn't Possibly Harm You," level and maintained a sense of humor, positive attitude, and open mind. I had learned so much during the Democratic Convention in New York the year Jimmy Carter was nominated. A friend put me in charge of the delegates from West Virginia. These people were scared to leave the hotel in "dangerous" New York City. They didn't realize that they intimidated me since I had no real knowledge of coal miners and tough union activists outside of the always-biased media. We were, in a sense, "on the same page." I encouraged them to ride subways and ask directions from strangers. They did. They told me how surprised they were that New Yorkers were so friendly! Their positive experiences liberated them from their fears and contact with them liberated me from any bias caused by the media.

My life was changing fast. Now South Dakota, not Soho, was my favorite destination.

So much had happened in three years. The Harmonic Convergence was in 1987. I tracked wolves and had my first vision on Bear Butte in '88, the same year Joe visited me in NYC and gave a Pipe Ceremony in my home. Early in '89 I painted the St Francis shrine in Vieques, Puerto Rico and in the summer found my way to the Snake River in the Sand Hills of Nebraska and then to the Sundance in Green Grass, South Dakota where I painted the first of many rock circles. And I continued to paint pictures and put on shows in New York. On top of it all, I had finally succeeded in quitting cigarettes. I felt I was living way beyond the speed limit but no one blew a whistle or gave me a ticket!

In the spring of 1990 Joe asked me if I would like to paint a circle of rocks in the Wilder Forest, a park near St. Paul where Native Americans could give ceremonies. This was an honor, especially because it was Joe who requested it. I knew in August I'd be painting another circle in Green Grass. I was eager to get my imagined web of stone circles underway but didn't know which way to go. North? South? Well, I went downtown to Joan Pancoe, of course, and into trance for a travel consultation. Together we did the special breathing that clears the way for communication with other realms. I popped into trance and right away saw a big bear looming over me. Joan said, in her flat matter-of-fact voice, "There's a large animal in the room," while I was mentally yelling, "No kidding!" Then I had the sensation that this bear spirit was pulling me, dragging me north. I felt like a vibrating compass needle. I saw a simplified map with a circle drawn over it. It went across North Dakota and circled around down through Montana. There it was, my itinerary. Not too specific but at least an idea! Barely, a map, so to speak. Sometimes, looking back, I marvel at how I learned to have faith in such things as phantom wolves and bears and how lovingly I embrace them.

My painted stone circles have had lives independent of me! A bear dismantled one I'd painted on a buffalo ranch in Halfway, Oregon. The rancher, Barbara Phillips, actually saw the bear sitting in the circle rolling the rocks around. My prayer became a bear playground and I was happy to imagine it. I was happier still when told the bear was probably foraging for grubs and other tasty delights under the stones. I had to keep watch for buffalo there and didn't know I needed to think about bears too.

While I was there, Barbara had to pen a buffalo bull that had an eye infection. She explained she hadn't known, when buying it, that long eyelashes are important for protecting the eyes of buffalo from flies. I "babysat" for that handsome fellow a couple of times by sitting at the edge of the pen and singing to him. He apparently liked it and would calm down. When painting on Barbara's ranch I sometimes found buffalo fluff stuck to tree trunks and I kept it. I have a roll of it in some buffalo hide that I call my "Buffalo Comfort Bundle." I hug it when I miss the Plains.

At Joe's invitation I painted the stone circle for the Wilder Forest and made it into a Medicine Wheel. A Medicine Wheel is a circle with two lines crossing through the diameter. One line connects north with south, the other connects east with west and they cross in the center of the circle. The cardinal directions have great philosophical meaning for all tribal people I know. For the directional lines I used small stones and painted stars on them. The stones forming the circle were painted with animals. I did a lot of the work at the house where Joe and his partner Sara were living. Having their company made it an even more rewarding and enriching experience.

The following year my medicine wheel was removed from Wilder by people who felt it wasn't authentically Native American which, of course, it wasn't, as I am not! Then, the year after that it was returned. I believed I was giving a simple prayer in visual terms but because of the perceptions of the time it became a political item. Though I am not Native American I wanted to be reassured that tobacco had been given to the stones when they were returned.

I had a lucky find in the Sand Hills, a pile of discarded slates. How delightful and easy it would be to paint on really flat stones. A friend in Rapid City had just asked me if I could paint a circle for her kindergarten. These slates would be perfect, so I loaded them into my van and drove off with a big smile.

When installing my painted circles I would always be sure the stones could stand so that rain would run off them and they wouldn't receive too much direct sun. Some stones could stand alone, but others needed what I called "helper rocks," for support. The flat slates needed those. When placed, they made a beautiful sight at that school. The little children, however, delighted in removing the "helpers" so they could stand on the animals. I didn't blame them one bit! I remembered an article in the New Yorker full of anecdotes about gorillas who liked to stand on people and I smiled a big one again!

A sect of the extreme Christian right later smashed these slates. What is menacing about a circle? Why are circles perceived to be a sign of evil? Was my prayer and celebration for the life of the Earth believed to be the work of the Devil by some people? Only the slate with the image of the bear survived, and to me, it was a reminder of what was important, Bear Butte, and the web of prayers I imagined emanating from it.

Birds seemed conspicuously absent in Nevada's Toiyabe Forest so I decided to paint them. I left a circle of eight stones with an extra one unpainted so that anyone finding the circle could imagine a bird that they would like to see there. I left a note to that effect with my address. Boy Scouts found this circle of birds and moved it to the Forest Ranger Center. They wrote to me appreciatively and wanted to know what my goal was.

Whatever happened to the stone circles, the little stone from Bear Butte was still in place, buried in the earth to connect the location energetically to the mountain, another strand in my own web of light!

That spring of 1990, needing rocks for the circle in the Wilder Forest, I realized for the first time it's not so easy to find smooth, river rocks the right size especially, it seemed, when I suddenly needed them. The rocks scattered by the ancient retreating glaciers were a gift to me, and a menace for farmers. Most farmers in Minnesota seemed to bury them or toss them in ditches and so they were hard to get at. One farmer had a stash near the road and when I slowed the van, invited me to take as many as I would like. "Wanna get rid of 'em, darned nuisance," he said.

In North Dakota, farmers piled unwanted stones in the middle of their fields and mowed and planted around them. The effect was often beautiful, sometimes humorous but even more difficult for me to access.

I got smart. Every time I found an accessible rock pile, or stream with the smooth rocks I needed, I stored them in my van, arranging them in lines around the sides of my sleeping bag. After a while they took on the aura of friendly companions. In fact, they all had stories to tell in their colors, their textures, compositions, scrapes, dents, and vibrations. I grew attached to some and I just kept them. When picking up stones, I always gave a pinch of tobacco in thanks to the earth, as Joe had taught me.

Following The Bear Itinerary

As I drove north through Minnesota following the bear's map, I had feelings of déjà vu. After a stop at a park with an exhibition of ice age artifacts, my mind was buzzing. I was sure I had once been a caribou hunter and that I was following an old route of migrating caribou. My New York persona, the skeptic, was saying "Yeah, sure, whatevah." But I was now also confident that it was possible to connect with lifetimes of the past. Somehow that makes all experience even richer. Then came the sudden thought: am I now creating memories or some kind of essence to be felt in future lives? Probably!

Circling west from Minnesota into North Dakota, I was submerged in fields of iridescent lavender-blue flax. I drank in this landscape and thirsted for more. North Dakota seemed flatter than the land of South Dakota and it felt like the horizon was at the edge of the planet. I could see competing thunderstorms to the northwest and to the south, with their separate huge thunderheads and lightning bolts. I wanted to run for cover fast, and so I sped north into the Turtle Mountains. In a poem I wrote about North Dakota, I said:

"Turtle Mountains, a land so sweet, bird song seeps in through your feet!"

Sweet it is with an abundance of birds. The chain of "potholes," (lakes or marshes,) I had become familiar with in the Sand Hills stretches from Canada into Kansas, so those white pelicans and other water birds were much in evidence. There were also a lot of turtles. No wonder the mountains were named after them! At that time of year, they were busy laying and burying their eggs, often in the middle of campsites. I had a lovely stash of stones that I thought of as pieces of Minnesota and began to paint in Turtle Mountain State Park.

When I was finished painting, I placed the circle of stones in a grassy spot near the entrance of the park. I painted animals native to the area. The Turtle Mountain Environmental Center moved my circle into the woods and made a trail to it. They used it, they said, as a teaching tool. Miss Earth Woman was pleased, actually thrilled! A few more green bangles were added to my lengthening robe of green sparkles.

As I crossed North Dakota, I wondered if anyone lived there, it was so untraveled. How could these wide-open spaces appear even wider, more open than what I had already experienced? Well, I hadn't been to the High Arctic yet!

The Bear Itinerary, as I thought of my journey, sent me into northeastern Montana. Here, the farmers were more helpful. They piled glacier-polished rocks in wire bins along the road. I loaded up and headed for Havre on the edge of the Bear Paw Mountains. I wasn't lost as I had feared. In the middle of North Dakota, the Bear Spirit was pointing the way. At the time there was no indication on the map or sign on the road to lead me to the largest county park in the United States, Beaver Creek Park in the Bear Paws. I asked an attendant in a gas station if there was any place to stay in the Bear Paws and that's how I found it.

I drove into the park and stopped at a little office near the entrance. The woman there said I could camp "up a ways," and could have a year's camping permit for ten dollars. Fine with me. She continued by warning me to be very careful and definitely not drive into the Indian reservation. She ranted on, saying the Indians were not really "their Indians," just Cree and Chippewa, that they were "breeds" who had gone begging at Fort Assinboine and were "given that land with the assumption they would die but they didn't!" I took this in, thanked her, and shocked by her venom, drove as far away as possible from the office and found a lovely spot to camp next to Beaver Creek. How comforting the voice of that little river was! I didn't see anyone else there nor did I see anyone along the road. I was a little anxious but believed I was in good hands. I should say, good "paws!" I remembered the photo of a bear that had fallen from my bookcase and felt reassured and thought about the bear I had experienced in trance.

How lucky Beaver Creek had some more rocks perfect for my purposes. I carried them to the picnic table near my van and cleaned them with a wire brush, getting mud out of cracks and removing moss. I lined them up to dry on the table and opened my book of animal silhouettes. I held the cutouts against their surfaces to decide what animal would fit compatibly. Is this stone a lion or a horse or…? Could this one be a swan? That stone looks ready for an elephant and on it went. Then I considered how stars would be worked in, large ones or small and how many. This was very consuming. I was completely absorbed and didn't know I had company until I looked up and saw two big policemen sauntering my way. Fear gripped my stomach and I could feel the adrenalin rise. They introduced themselves as the Sheriff and a State Trooper and they could not have been nicer. They said they were curious, just wanted to know what I was doing. Probably wondering what kind of dangerous nut would be up there all alone. They said they'd stop by now and then to be sure I was okay. They told other people about me and I had some wonderful visitors who brought rocks, food, good conversation, and encouragement. I was having such a good time that I kept on painting and the circle of twenty stones I had planned for the Bear Paw Mountains grew larger and larger until there were thirty stones. I also painted special stones for some of my visitors. A wonderful couple, Ray and Anna, were camped down the road. They were in Havre for a family reunion. They were great animal lovers and so enthusiastic about what I was doing that I painted a special stone for them. Then there was Doc and Cora, a couple in their eighties who arranged for this big circle to be installed in front of the Kiwanis Chapel. In the center of it I painted a large rock with a quote from an old Sioux Bear Song, "My paw is sacred, everything is sacred." It seemed perfect in the Bear Paw Mountains! Doc said, "You're just like a spider, always working." I was tempted to reply with, "How did you know?" Part of my private prayer there was that the destruction of those mountains for ore would come to an end. I think a lot of people felt the same.

I forgot about the Indian Reservation until I saw an Indian roaring down the road in his pickup with his horse standing in the back. And I swear that horse was laughing. He was getting a ride instead of being ridden! Doc confirmed that horse enjoyed riding standing up in the back of the pickup and the faster the better. He was a local celebrity.

I did drive up to the "Rocky Boy" reservation just to look around. Beautiful country, but that could be said about nearly every inch of Montana. When I got back to my campsite I discovered with horror that a pair of black panties I'd washed in the creek were still hanging from the windshield wipers in my rear window. I hoped no one had seen them. Well, at least they were dry.

It was hard to leave the Bear Paws and all those fine people but I moved on, drove south bypassing the Bear Tooth Mountains and circled into Wyoming to Devil's Tower, roughly following the route shown by that spirit bear in trance. Devil's Tower was once named Bear's Lodge and was very sacred to the bands of the Sioux. It seems many places sacred to the natives were later given names that included "hell" or "devil" but I don't want to speculate on the reasons for this. Although the Tower is a popular tourist destination, the trails around it and the adjacent forest were nearly empty and I enjoyed them all. I phoned my daughter, Deirdre, in California, raving on about my journey until, in a reversal of roles, she interrupted me to ask, "Mom, when was the last time you had a bath?" I honestly couldn't remember and went immediately to the bathhouse in the campground. I'd forgotten how good a hot shower can feel!

And then, it was just a short hop into South Dakota and to Bear Butte. Many times during my journeys I received beautiful messages in my dreams such as, "The rainbow begins at your feet, you have only to follow it," and "No act of the heart ever fails," and "Love illumines the way." It seemed some kind spirit was often there encouraging me with valentines.

This time I approached Bear Butte from the north, the mountain rising from the flat expanse of the plains like a large ship at sea. I felt awe, excitement, and profound love. I decided to spend another night up top.

I visited Bear Butte many times over twelve years and each visit was unique. When I began the winding switchback trail up from the campground I felt I was entering a temple. The path is not too steep at first. It moves gently up from the campground to a saddle in the mountain with a wide-open view to the north. The grassy slope there is just right for sitting in meditation or basking in the sunlight. From there the trail turns back and becomes a narrow ledge through a rockslide looking down on the campground with its sweat lodge. It climbs to a wooden platform where you can rest and look south to the peaks of the Black Hills.

It continues upward through forest to an open area with a rock ledge and a little cave where that large porcupine lived. I always hoped to see it again and addressed it as "grandfather" when I did. Getting nearer to the top there was another wooden platform looking, forever it seemed, into the North. You could see a butte named "Deer's Ears" because its silhouette looked just like that. The trail then backtracks and there is a little path climbing up to some rocks and a couple of trees looking east. That somewhat precipitous place was my favorite perch. It was open to the stars and the glorious sunrise. Prayer flags were often there, and sometimes offerings of feathers so I knew vision quests took place there.

The main trail then continues steeply to the summit and that is where I spent the night, looking out over the Black Hills in the distance, hoping the lightning I saw above them wouldn't move in my direction. Nothing special happened that night, except that I was happy, I was on Bear Butte, the sacred mountain, and felt that I truly belonged. I felt comforted and far from the anguish of the world. What could be better than that! In my journal I reported "remarkable winds from many directions, a sweet grass wind, a soft pine wind, wet earth wind, storms in the west circling north from an orange sunset dotted by black islands."

In the morning, when I stood up to greet the rising sun, a small spider jumped into my hand. I held out my palm with fingers outspread and watched this minute and precious creature spin a web across my fingers going from one to the next. It was black with a white dot on its back and had yellow legs. I nearly drowned it in tears! I gave a pinch of tobacco to the earth and gave thanks for this greeting from another small web spinner. And I thanked this mountain as my spiritual teacher and mother.

As I descended the mountain, a rockslide below me suddenly lit up. The rising sun had illuminated all the strands of spider silk running from one rock to another, a mirror of what I had seen in the heavens two years before. And I believed this was an affirmation for me, that all my rock circles were connected to each other and to the mountain too.

I am always learning about the connectedness of all things and surprised, over and over again, always wondering what I am supposed to do with what I've learned. I once met a member of the Shinnecock tribe. He looked very troubled when he saw me. He said he had seen me in a dream as a teacher from the stars! Well, not that I know of. But maybe that's what all of us really are!

The Second Sundance
And An Unusual Artist

*I*t was good to be back in Green Grass again, in spite of the dust that clogs your pores, stiffens your hair, and gets caught in your teeth. The drought wasn't over yet.

This year, at the end the third day of the Sundance, Vincent Black Feather, the attending medicine man, conducted a healing in the dance ring for supporters of the dancers. We lined up outside the east entrance to the dance area and one by one entered to have our heads and shoulders brushed by his large eagle feather as a blessing. We all felt refreshed. As we waited our turns, we looked up and saw small clouds form the word "LOEV." The E was backwards, the letters were all capitals on the same scale, just out of order. There were no other clouds in the sky, no skywriting planes, simply this message written clearly though inaccurately spelled, above us. Who or what was sending love to us?

As the year before, the White Buffalo Calf Pipe bundle was brought out in a special ceremony at the end of the Sundance. Everyone collected bunches of sage to make a path from the Pipe House to a spot downhill where the Pipe would be laid on a buffalo robe. There was a breath taking moment when Arvol Looking Horse, carrying the Pipe bundle, and Rufus in his buffalo regalia, flanked by two riders wearing feathers in their hair, wielding eagle feather staffs, suddenly appeared at the top of the hill, then slowly descended on the path of sage to the beat of the big drum.

My status in Green Grass had improved when it was learned that I was over fifty years of age. That made me an elder, not just a "white woman." Elders are respected and invited to be the first to pray with the ancient Pipe by kneeling next to it and putting their hands on the buffalo fur bundle that holds it. And we were first to shake the hand of Arvol Looking Horse who stood next to it. As usual I was a bit overcome, nearly tripping over the buffalo robe and stumbling into Arvol. I can never be dignified when I want to be.

At the close of the Sundance, attended by more people this time, Robert Grey Bear introduced me to people at the HV Johnston Sioux Cultural Center in Eagle Butte. They wondered what I had planned for their children. I had shipped out big rolls of paper and a box of paint, glitter, yarn, feathers and glue. As an artist and occasional art teacher, I knew kids loved making full- sized self-portraits. They begin by lying down on a large sheet of paper to be outlined. Then materials are introduced, a few suggestions made, such as, you may paint yourself as you are, or would like to be, or you can pretend you are an animal, a robot, an extraterrestrial, and so forth.

The Sioux children were reserved at first but quickly got involved. A lot of them had already been using the art supplies I had in my camp during the Sundance. They asked if they could glitter their sneakers and I said, "Go for it but I hope your parents aren't mad at me." This didn't worry them a bit.

The next day I rolled out a long length of paper, and placed jars of paint down the middle of it. There were twenty children sitting on the floor, ten on either side. I asked them to paint whatever they liked and promised they would later see what a wonderful picture they made together even if they hadn't planned it. These children were such a pleasure. There was never any fighting over brushes or paint colors. They knew how to share. It was a natural part of their lives.

Well, we were having a fine time laughing and chattering, when all of a sudden a large white dog appeared. There was a collective intake of breath as he paused, then stood for a second at the end of the paper, before casually trotting its length, knocking over a jar of red paint. He walked through the paint leaving an array of red footprints that artfully centered the composition, (so to speak). Some adults rushed in saying, "Oh, we are so sorry. He heard the children having such a good time, we could not stop him." I gave a wink and speaking in a tone of authority, said, "We do not often have visiting dog artists and we are happy he could join us." I looked at their faces and the children's faces. There was a pause and then the biggest smiles you've ever seen. That communal painting was special and I enjoyed feeling a part of the community outside the Sundance Ceremony.

Grey Bear and I subsequently became pals. I called him "Grey Bear" not "Robert, because he was as rare as a grey bear must be. He even came to New York a couple of times to give Pipe ceremonies. Rosy loved him, as did other regulars at our Pipe Ceremonies. When we visited the displays of Indian artifacts and medicine bundles in the Natural History Museum and Metropolitan Museum he would pull out his tobacco pouch and give a little offering. Wherever I went with Grey Bear, there was a trail of tobacco. When we drove from South Dakota to Oregon one time, tobacco streamed from the windows of the car. We were always giving thanks for something, and that is a wonderful way to live!

Another Night On Bear Butte

*I*believed I had completed the "Bear Itinerary" but that bear spirit wouldn't let me go. I kept having the unsettled feeling that comes when something is not quite right, not complete. It's a feeling very familiar to me. When I'm working on a painting that's not quite "there," I have a sense of vague physical unease. I believed I 'd followed the circle the bear had pointed out. I also read about bears and all that I could find of their indigenous songs and stories. I looked at their many splendid representations in art and sculpture and visited them in the zoo. I painted them on many rocks and designed a popular T-shirt called "Bear Dance." I joined groups protecting bears. Still, something nagged. It was as if that Bear Spirit had alerted something indefinable in my spirit.

Bears and wolves were often in my thoughts. It was fun to be walking down Park Avenue to a lecture at the Asia society wanting to howl, or thinking about the Bear Spirit on the bus to Lincoln Center or sitting in the subway wondering where the old deer paths had been on Manhattan. I liked to think that I was sneaking the wilds back to the city. And I thought about the city in a new context. I felt its huge energy grew from the crystal-like mica-filled stone it was built on and that the flocks of rock doves (pigeons) circling it continuously brought about a balance of energies like two opposing yet harmonious themes in a piece of music.

I thought about the powerful presence of wolves and bears in so much of the world, and their longstanding relationships with humans. They have been friend, foe, teacher, guide, food and clothing for eons. The truth is, they are family. And as much a manifestation of the nature of planet Earth as humans are.

In 1991, the third year of the Sundance in Green Grass, I followed what I now thought of as my usual route, a brief stay in St Paul, with visits to friends, renting another Vanita von Van, then heading south to Luverne with a turkey dinner at the Blue Mound Inn and on to the cabin on the Snake River in Nebraska's Sand Hills. I had favorite roads and vistas that I looked forward to and sometimes had to giggle at myself, the New Yorker who now reveled in the wide open spaces and their long empty roads and felt so at home.

I am a Sagittarius, the sign of the traveler, but my rising sign is Virgo, sign of the homebody. This has sometimes led to a kind of "go-stay, stay-go" conflict but more often than not, it's helped me to feel at home almost everywhere I have been. For me, feeling "at home," means establishing connections not only with other people in a given location, but the land itself, its plant and animal life, and partaking in a meaningful enjoyment of it all.

Magnum Blatt, the chocolate retriever at the Snake River Hunting and Fishing Club, greeted me with frenzied doggy joy and I expressed the human kind. It seemed he and I were the only ones who ever hiked the Snake River. Though one time on my own I was surprised to come across two fishermen and I didn't like the way they looked at me. Suddenly when one of them got a bite on his line I quickly scooted up a hidden trail Magnum had discovered the week before.

Sometimes I drove Magnum to Merritt Lake and we ran along the beach and explored dunes and pools. I enjoyed identifying animal tracks and he enjoyed sniffing them. I was simply happy with my buddy, Magnum. But after a few weeks I got restless, gave my deliciously smelly sneakers to Magnum for company, and drove off. I wanted to spend another night on Bear Butte before going to the third Sundance. I also needed some stones for my next circle in Green Grass and I knew a riverbed not far from the mountain, which had supplied me with smooth, paintable stones before.

I took a little-used road from the Snake River into the Badlands and stayed in one of the tiny one-room cabins in Cedar Pass. The cabins were located in a little oasis with trees full of conversing magpies and rabbits hopping below. Nearby was one of my favorite trails that climbs and twists upward and includes a ladder to reach spectacular views of the colorful Badlands sunsets. It was where I had found that twiggy plant I'd seen in a vision. It was the one that introduced itself as "fingers of the earth." In fact, it was called the "skeleton plant" because it doesn't have leaves. I read that it is useful with eye problems. And I learned that its roots can go as far as six feet into the Earth and thought perhaps that was the reason for the special energy it had transmitted into my hands at the close of the first Sundance. Why had that plant "spoken" to me? Did I have looming eye problems, or maybe I wasn't "seeing" things as clearly or deeply as I might. Then it occurred to me that I might become "fingers of the earth," a person with healing hands. Surely this land had seen me before and I was grateful to be roaming it again. Maybe I had unfinished business here. Could my restlessness relate to the Bear Spirit I felt was close by, still, in a sense, whispering to me. Perhaps an earlier lifetime here was cut short. I always felt and still do, that I am a student in an extraordinary and mysterious university. I thought again that while I was sensing a past life, perhaps I was also laying groundwork for another lifetime, the one to come. The Badlands is a cathedral for reflection! A voice in a dream said the Badlands "are old, even to itself."

From the Badlands I drove to the Black Hills, stopped in Blackhawk for a visit with Joanie and her children. I continued to Bear Butte, taking the back road out of Sturgis for that thrilling first view of the mountain. It vibrates with energy. It's easy to believe that it is indeed a sleeping bear, a very big one. I took the road on the mountain to the parking lot for those who are there for spiritual reasons and walked across the little bridge from the parking lot to the Sweat Lodge area on the mountain's side. When I sat beneath a tree to catch my breath, a flock of bluebirds arrived and bustled around in the branches above me. What a beautiful welcome! I believed the mountain was happy to have me back.

I walked the trail to the top, always giving pinches of tobacco in thanks along the way and always taking note of the life along the trail, especially birds who always have significance for me. Sometime during a very peaceful night I heard a little melody. It was very brief. I kept waiting for more but nothing came. It was sweet but frustrating because it didn't seem complete. What could it mean? Where was it from? I believed this little melody must be meaningful because I had, after all, heard it while on the mountain, my teacher.

With that as yet understood little melody still clinging to my brain, I drove away from Bear Butte and headed for Green Grass to attend the third Sundance. At the conclusion of it Arvol Looking Horse once again brought out the Buffalo Calf Pipe bundle. This year I was asked to paint four stones in the colors of the four directions to mark the area. Then with drums beating we all spread out across a wide field and danced in place. What ecstasy it was to be dancing on that sweet smelling land to the powerful vibration of the big drum. It would have been easy to slip into trance.

While dancing I looked down in the space next to me and saw a feather. It was an eagle feather and it stood upright, its quill stuck in the earth. It quivered. It looked like it was dancing too. It wasn't there when I started dancing so I looked around thinking someone would be running to catch it after it had blown away. I imagined it must belong to someone there until I suddenly realized that I was that someone! I picked it up and, still dancing, felt its cool silk against my cheek. Its pattern suggested that a piece of cloud had fallen into my hands. What wonder I experienced.

A Paiute woman from Nevada also received a feather then and loudly trilled her joy. How I wished I could ululate like that. Joe had once told me that eagle feathers are earned. This eagle feather and the one from Scott Lupi hang from the Pipe I was later given. It was my third eagle feather but not my last.

Spiraling Out

You're completing a circle, Claire and soon you will begin to spiral out." Joan made this comment while we had lunch in an East Village restaurant looking out over the exotic human parade there.

"That sounds exciting, Joan," I said, "but I hope I won't be spiraling as far out as some of these neighbors of yours."

But Joan's prediction became true repeatedly and began with a journey to Peru and the Amazon in 1990, followed by Africa in '91, Russia in '92, Egypt in '93, the Canadian High Arctic in '94, with summers across the continent, punctuated by returns to Vieques for a show of my paintings, vacations with my two daughters and to help after hurricane Hugo. Most trips were financially possible because political unrest greatly reduced the cost of travel. Lucky for me, and my friends, we received the benefits of these journeys without experiencing any of the feared problems.

The little melody I'd heard on the mountain had remained a mystery. I'd begun to doubt that I'd even heard it. I had almost given up trying to understand what it was when less than a year later I "spiraled out" to Moscow, Russia.

The government of Russia had just changed hands. Plane tickets were cheap. People were hesitant to travel. Who knew what could happen. But some friends and I decided to take advantage of the lowered fares.

On the first morning there, from a window in a hotel owned by Gorbachev, we heard sounds coming from a church across the street. The churches had just been reopened. We went to see if there was a service in progress. The church was crowded. There were no pews. The Priests stood singing the Mass amid clouds of incense rising from the swinging silver censers. There came a pause in the litany when the congregation sang a response to the Priests. What they sang was the very same melody I had heard on top of Bear Butte! I burst into tears. It was as though I had received a physical blow. I could scarcely believe it. How was this possible?

When I finally met that great medicine man, Martin High Bear in 1993, whose name I had heard six years before, I told him the story. Slowly, in his rough, scratchy voice he said, "Well now, you see, the earth is all one. It's all one piece." He opened his arms and made a circle with his hands, then pointed, "What happens here, well, you can feel it there. You see?" I could feel this understanding growing and pressing against my skull.

My friends and I joined an extraordinary journey by a boat down the Volga River from Moscow to Kazan. There were only twenty-five of us on a boat for three hundred. There was a small group of English art historians who wanted to see if any art remained in the newly reopened churches, a few Lutheran farmers from Minnesota hoping to find ways to revitalize lands damaged by over use of chemical fertilizers, and then there was my group, artists and actors from NYC.

It was a journey that I rated on a scale of one to ten handkerchiefs a day because I cried every day. I cried at the plight of hungry, isolated people, land destroyed by chemicals, and the lifeless river. I tear up thinking about it even now. But there was also joy, especially in the way we bonded with the ship's crew. Many of them were very young. Some expressed concern about who would care for their small patch of land while they were on board because it was where they grew the potatoes that kept their families from starving. This startled us and helped us understand the meals on board the "Russ" and why all were served with radishes and cucumbers. On one memorable occasion we were served tongue. On another we were each given a piece of lettuce. The cooks did wonders with the little food available—potato soup with sturgeon, cottage cheese pudding, sprats in oil and proudly created meringues to delight us.

And there was joy in how we were greeted in many stops along the river, especially at Nizhni Novgorod, where Sakharov the great physicist had been imprisoned. There was a great outcry of excitement when people there learned Americans were present. We were not at all sure how we would be regarded or if we would be welcome. We did "high fives" all the way down the street. Some a cappella singers sang for us in a ruined church. We enjoyed them so much the captain of the boat took them on board so they could continue singing while we cruised around the area. I was able to find stones along the river. These stones and others brought on board by crew members were really rubble from centuries of destruction and reuse, not at all the smooth river rocks of America's streams and rivers. Of course I had my book of animal cut outs and was so pleased to paint a circle for the earth in Russia. In the forest that became the destination for this circle, I found a mysterious offering of eggshell painted red wrapped in red cloth with a bit of tobacco. What was its significance? I felt it was a kind of affirmation for me, and an indication of perhaps indigenous spiritual life in that area.

There was a small celebration for the rock circle when I finished painting it. The kitchen staff carried a fine lunch to a site surrounded by trees. It was adjacent to a three-story cement high rise that was a vacation retreat designated by the government as a reward for those who had done good work. The boat's engineer had his pet cat with him and carried it on land so it could see the stones that honored animals. Zina, our lively guide, pointed at the wild dogs arriving and declared, "You see, they understand it is for them, for the animals." The crew shared their bread with insistent ravens and Earth Woman twinkled greenly.

Our next stop was in the small city of Yaroslavl where some artists led us to their "cooperative" on a high floor of a crumbling cement building. They were drawing with turkey feather quills. They gave me one and I treasure it and the memory of those cheerful artists who worked in the cold with very little light. There I bought a small drawing of a thoughtful looking wolf towering over the rooftops of a village.

In one village, we conversed with a man who felt sorry for us because he believed Russia was so advanced. He assumed we were there to learn how we might make our lives better.

We were in Moscow on the day people were permitted for the first time to sell possessions publicly in the street. It was painful to see how ill at ease they were and that their possessions were so meager. At the wonderful Tolstoy home/museum the young men in charge were thrown into confusion when I offered a donation. When I insisted that it was for the care of the building and grounds they gave me an old photo of the bearded Tolstoy. It's a classic and a treasure. In Red Square, young people gave us a flag they had made with their names on it and asked us not to forget them. I don't think we ever will.

At the end of the journey when we left the boat in a bus for the airport, all of us waving with our faces pressed against the windows, the waving, weeping crew started running after us. Oh, we laughed, these emotional Russians! In fact, the luggage compartment at the side of the bus had opened and our luggage was beginning to tumble out. This was a great moment of shared hilarity!

In Russia I awoke to how governments, for their own selfish purposes, manipulate the opinions of people about each other. I learned that it is the old women who quietly and secretly guard the artifacts of spiritual tradition and preserve them for new generations. I learned that music and the arts cannot be held down and that people of the heart will connect no matter what their languages or appearances or histories may be. I thought about the threads of light connecting stars I'd seen from Bear Butte. Didn't that suggest infinite possibilities for connection, for interrelatedness?

Loving Gorillas And An Eagle

My younger daughter Madeleine has a very insistent personality and I'm a bit of a pushover, so when she called one morning and said, "I'm going to Africa, Mom and you're coming with me, you have to," I hemmed and hawed just for form's sake. She was working on a book for children called *Here is the African Savannah* and wanted to see the real thing.

She was an "Earth Woman" long before me, already talking about "planet consciousness" at the age of twelve. My response at the time was a distracted, "What a nice idea, Sweetheart!"

I doubted I could paint any stone circles at our African destinations since we would be camping in the grasslands of the Serengeti, the home of lions and leopards and others that might view me as a meal. So I wondered if there was any special purpose for me there. As usual I went to my favorite travel agent, Joan. In trance she described a prehistoric lifetime on the African continent, and while I was unable to "see" it I felt it and it felt very dark, damp, thick with vegetation, and suffocating. I'm not sure I was human. "Mmmm," said Joan, "Ah yes, oh my, you sacrificed your life to save your people. You gave your life for them, Claire, and you were promised..." Then suddenly, "Oh my god, Claire you're going to get your power back in the middle of Africa!" Joan couldn't see what that meant, just that it would happen.

"Power" wasn't anything I'd ever imagined. I associated it only with male institutions and earthquakes. And I didn't think about this prediction at all once I got there. Africa was far too enthralling!

The morning of our arrival in Arusha, Tanzania, I walked out onto the verandah of the hotel and was greeted by a dwarf, who said, in a very low voice, "Jambo, Mama!" I was immediately captivated. And later delighted when our guide, Willi Hombo greeted elephants, lions, and birds with that same glad sounding Swahili word, "jambo!"

Madeleine and I were among the last fortunate few permitted to camp at the edge of the Lerai Forest at the bottom of the Ngorogoro Crater. At night, the eyes of small wild cats surrounding our camp glowed in the light from our fire. At dawn we joined the hunt of lionesses.

The Crater is given over entirely to birds and animals and we were living among them, in their powerful abundance, on their land. Here we felt the great joyful laughter of creation triumphant, of the paradise of which we were once a part. I wept over the lions and Madeleine wept over the elephants. To experience some small sense of their lives moved us deeply. The variety, beauty and numbers of birds astonished us and so did our guide, Msheeza, who had memorized the East African bird guide and could tell us on what page any given species could be found!

The Serengeti revealed so much of its life to us.

At a territorial line invisible to us, we witnessed two pairs of male cheetahs challenging each other, leaping with enormous grace and chirruping like birds. Two lone males watched at a distance. The conflict was resolved when one of the pairs slowly edged away, turning back every so often. Willi Hombo was anxious throughout this encounter because he feared it would become violent and cheetahs would be killed, leaving fewer on that great land.

Later that day Willi dazzled us when he spotted at a great distance, a leopard sleeping in a tree. He explained that a branch hanging at an unnatural angle from a tree in the distance is often the drooping limb of a sleeping leopard. We quietly approached in our van for a view of this magnificent creature and returned in the evening to watch it descend the tree for an evening hunt. The power emanating from its rippling muscles made us acutely aware of our terrible human vulnerability.

Even though roaring lions and coughing hyenas near our tents at night could be frightening, we missed them when we left the Serengeti. Camping in a school soccer field seemed a bit tame, though meeting with teachers and students was a friendly and warm exchange that gave us insight into the human life of Tanzania.

The students were so curious about us they followed us to the toilet and the teachers apologized because their schoolhouse was not a modern cement one. To this we expressed sincere admiration for their mud brick structures and said there was more than enough cement in the world! Everyone seemed to have sniffles. It gets quite cold at night. I imagined having a truck full of knitting supplies and teaching everyone across the country to knit scarves and blankets.

Our next destination was Zaire, (now The Democratic Republic of the Congo) where we hoped to see gorillas. In the 60's I had been moved by George Schaller's book *Year of the Gorilla* and here we were, about to enter one of the few places they still lived. I could see that Willi Hombo was nervous when our van was stopped at the border. The customs officer who boarded it looked surly. In essence, Willi warned us to "keep a low profile," but the open windows of our vehicle invited communication with the curious crowd peering at us. I overheard some French, so I began a conversation, reached in my purse, and brought out a gift I had brought to express thanks and/or smooth over difficult transitions. It was a bag of blue marbles with a tiny green maps of the planet painted on them. When I pointed to the miniscule map on the marble and said, "You are here" and then pointed to North America saying, "We are from here," all the tension in the air evaporated and with smiles we were waved through the border. (I frequently gave this marble away in journeys across North America with the words, "Now the Earth is in your hands.")

We stayed in tents in an open area in the jungle. Early in the hot and steamy morning we began an uphill hike into this land of extinct volcanoes where we hoped to meet gorillas. Our guide produced sticks of dynamite. He said he would use them if wild elephants charged us. The elephants did not appear but the gorillas did and we spent some brief sweet time with them. As our guide explained, they cannot tolerate human company for more than half an hour. I guess the human vibration is just too frantic, too intense for them.

A male gorilla suddenly appeared on the trail. He and the guide exchanged some grunts. Our guide beckoned and we followed him a short way into the jungle. He instructed us to move slowly, quietly and to crouch down, sit on the earth and casually pretend to munch on leaves. We were told to look harmless but I don't think we fooled the gorillas one bit. They know what kind of animals we are. We are a dangerous species. The guide warned that a female gorilla who actually liked people might make an appearance and to remain cool and relaxed if she approached us. She did appear and sat down behind Madeleine and began undoing her braid and plucked at her scalp as if grooming her. All the while silent tears were streaming down Madeleine's cheeks, not from pain but from that intense joy we feel when a member of another species seems to like us. A youngster appeared. It had lost a hand in a skirmish with a rival gorilla clan. Although gorillas are peaceful, they do have occasional territorial clashes. This little one started to come to me and the large male who was lying down in front of us grunted a warning and the little one rapidly retreated to his side. We humans would happily have spent more than half an hour with these gorillas because there was something deeply liberating in sharing their lives in that mountain jungle, even so very briefly.

The people attending our campsite were very kind. We saw that they were achingly poor. Madeleine and I wondered how we could help them and suggested to the group that they leave any extra shoes. Our tour was ending so we no longer needed extra shoes or other items. Suddenly a young couple who had been very nice but retiring said, "Oh don't do that, it will encourage them to breed."

We were so stunned by this statement our jaws literally dropped open. This couple seemed instantly confused and agitated as though they had really heard this litany taught them, wherever they came from, for the very first time. Isn't it good to occasionally think about what dictates you unconsciously accept from your culture, religion or government? I hope this couple did! What they expressed was a classic example of the "Us and Them" syndrome that has plagued the world for as long as life has been upon it. It seems that many tribal names when translated, mean, "The People." If you are not a member of "The People" you are less than human and it seems there is no limit to the suffering that can be inflicted upon you. Does your nation, culture or religion insist that you are "The People" and others are not?

Our next destination was the Hotel du Lac on Lake Tanganyika in Bujumbura, Burundi. I hadn't given Joan's prediction that I would recover my "power" any thought at all until looking at the map of our journey. The map indicated we were pretty much in the middle of Africa.

The Hotel du Lac was spread out over large gardens and it had a disturbing "zoo" reminiscent of some of the worst roadside zoos in the U.S. The animals, including chimps and dik-diks, were frightened and disoriented. I don't think anyone really knew how to take care of them. It was painful to see and I tried to avoid these cages but was drawn repeatedly to that of the African Fishing Eagle. It looked similar to the North American Bald Eagle though its white throat seemed longer and its beak appeared to have a more pronounced hook. It was utterly still, and no wonder. That cage was too small for it to spread its wings. It seemed hunched in silent despair but emanated the vibration of power in terrible restraint.

I bent to put a small stone from Bear Butte in its cage and offer a prayer. As I stood up, our eyes met. Those penetrating golden eyes shot through me, cracked open my heart and I began to sing in a way I had never sung before. A channel between my heart and voice had sprung open and the sound tore through me becoming a long lament that reached out to embrace this bird. Then that great eagle flung back its head and its long piercing cries rang out over the hotel grounds. I didn't know that African fishing eagles were famous for their haunting cries or that this eagle had been mute since captivity, and I was stunned.

Workers in the gardens and from the hotel rushed over. They were excited. One of them asked me where I was from and I replied in French, the commonly used language there, "Amerique du Nord." I could hear this information being repeated. They studied me and saw the beaded medicine pouch I wore at the time and looked at each other with knowing glances. They became very respectful and they wanted to touch me. Something of the mantle of the priestess or medicine woman must have descended upon me for a moment and I knew intuitively it was what these people needed and I rose to the occasion. I declared, "Le bon dieu aime les aigles. Dans mon pays nous chantons toujours aux aigles." (The good god loves the eagles. In my country we always sing to the eagles.) I took a breath and continued with passion in my voice because I knew I was speaking out for the life force of this fellow creature. "Qui chantera a ce grand oiseau quand je ne suis plus ici?" (Who will sing to this great bird when I am not here?) There were murmurs and as drama seemed to dictate, at the moment I finished speaking, the eagle shook itself and

Eric and me

Bear Butte, SD

My perch on top of Bear Butte

The Crow Fair in Montana

Robert Grey Bear

Galen Drapeau, a chief and spiritual leader of the Yankton Sioux tribe

Joe Geshick, superb artist of the Ojibway, (photo, courtesy of Sara Remke)

That gorgeous Apache, Rosy (photo courtesy of Jane Walker Richmond)

Claire among the pyramids of Giza, Egypt

Zaire now again the Congo

Members of the Quileute tribe wearing my T-shirts in La Push, Wa.

Hugging a giant spruce tree in Haida Gwaii (formerly Queen Charlotte Islands)

Isabel Ides, famous storyteller and basket maker of the Makah tribe in Neah Bay Wa.

Isabel Ides and grandson looking at the circle I painted for her

Engineer and cat of the Russ, Volga River boat, Russia

My buddy, Magnum, at the Snake River Hunting and Fishing Club, Nebraska, as a puppy and as an adult.

Altar of St. Francis at the Casa del Frances in Vieques, PR

Green Grass, SD

Green Grass, SD

Rock circle in progress

Show at Phoenix Gallery in New York City

Show at the Summer Song Gallery in Seattle - Circle of Sea Life

View from the bridge of Russian ice cutter Klebnikov, Canadian High Arctic

Claire painting stones for the Resolute school, in her cabin aboard the Klebnikov

shed a big black wing feather that fell into the dirty water pan below. A man opened the cage, reached in for the feather and gave it to me, my fourth eagle feather.

When I returned to our small cottage, Madeleine was standing in the doorway looking concerned. "What's all the commotion, Mom?" I hardly knew where to begin but within a minute some of the garden workers showed up carrying the pan of water with eagle urine from the cage. I thanked them but had no idea what they thought I would do with it. "What is that stinking stuff, Mom?" Well, I did my best to describe all that had transpired and said I imagined that eagle urine might, to some people, be like Holy Water is to others. We flopped down on the beds and sank into silence. Finally, Madeleine spoke, "Listen Mom, this IS the middle of Africa and Joan doesn't joke around. I think you just got your power back and that it is this voice from your heart. I really think that's it."

Power Of A Feather

Wandering the Sand Hills I sometimes sang because the land seemed to call for it, but this was different. It was a powerful current of love and compassion charging through me. What had the eagle felt? When I thought about the eagle I thought of it as "my heart" and I gave it that name in French, "Mon Coeur."

When I next saw Robert Grey Bear in Eagle Butte I told him about the eagle and how I had been moved to sing. There's nothing he likes more than a good laugh, so my story was greeted with, "Eheheheeehahaeehha," that laughter of his that's like a long extended chortle/chuckle. "Oh," he said, "your heart was pierced! You should meet Marilyn. Her heart was pierced in a dream by a dolphin. He told her how his nation is suffering, and she can't stop telling people about it either, Claire." Still laughing he said, "And you're blessed when that happens, you're blessed. And that singing, that's called heart singing though some say it is really the earth who sings." Then changing his demeanor, he asked, "Does the Earth lament the pain of her children?"

That evening Grey Bear led a sweat lodge ceremony, and when it was time for water to be passed around, I asked if I might sing for it. I had suddenly seen water in a different way, how magical it is, how precious it is and out came a truly beautiful song. After the ceremony people asked me about it, where did the song come from, what was the name of it? All I could say was that it came from my heart and I wouldn't know how to repeat it.

Only later as I more often found the need to express myself by singing did I really think of this singing as a power being returned to me. It has opened doors to many adventures and best of all has become a healing tool that has helped to dispel pain and fear in many places in the world and has been a welcome addition in many ceremonies. I even had the honor of singing for Aboriginal boys going on Walkabout.

In the spring, the feather from the African Fishing Eagle, "Mon Coeur," turned out to be a kind of passport. My friend Christina, whom I had met on the Earthwatch Wolf Tracking project, sent out an SOS. She had gotten involved with an Ojibwa medicine man who left her stranded in his brother's home in Bemidji in northern Minnesota when he left for a ceremony in North Dakota. Could I please come and get her? Yes, of course, and easy to do since I was already in St. Paul. I reached Bemidji after dark and stayed in a nice inexpensive room in the dormitory of the college there.

Next morning, I found the house and a very relieved-to-see-me Christina, who must have been standing by the door it opened so fast. I entered the sitting room and caught my breath, not because of the four rather dour men sitting there, but because of all the eagle feather regalia around the room. There were bonnets, staffs, and fans, and individual feathers with beaded quills. I'd never seen anything like this. My mouth was probably hanging open but I was invited to sit down. A heavy silence followed. I'd already learned that most Natives do not converse for the sake of conversation but I wanted to connect, so I said in my bright social voice, that I had recently met an eagle in Africa. That it was an eagle with a haunting voice. Studying the many feathers around the room I mentioned that it had given me a feather. There was a slight stir of interest.

"Do you have it? Do you have the feather?" asked one of the men. "Yes, of course, it's in my van. Would you like to see it?" Affirmative nods. I brought it in wrapped in red cloth with some tobacco.

The feather was passed around, each man studying it for quite a time. It slowly dawned on me that this might be some sort of test. Perhaps the vibration from the feather provided answers to questions they didn't care to ask. At last one of them smiled and he said while nodding, "You are welcome here." Another said, "You can visit us any time." Big smiles all around and Christina and I made a graceful exit. It was then that Christina told me that the men who inspected my eagle feather were all members of the famous Midewiwin Medicine Society. It can take a lifetime to be fully initiated into this very prestigious society. What had they seen? What had they learned from my precious eagle feather that made me welcome? The following year the head of Midewiwin, Archie Mosey, was invited to a Lakota Sundance hosted by Galen Drapeau. I was there to see him arrive. It was a significant moment because his arrival indicated the "traditional enemy" status of Ojibwa and Lakota was coming to an end. Ancient hostilities were their only weapons, but as recent history around the world shows, they can be the most dangerous.

Return Of The Bear Spirit

Whenever I returned to the Snake River after a Sundance, my body was so full of electrical energy that lamps flickered and radios crackled, bringing some sizzle to the old Hunting and Fishing Club. It became a bit of a joke between Bill and me. "Charged up?" he said when my dusty van once again pulled into the club. "You bet I am" I replied, "but it's this cold wind that's making me shiver!" Bill laughed and remarked, "Fall's comin' early this year. Nighthawks, already bunchin'up."

And that, I thought, is what wolves do too. In summer they can roam alone. In autumn they start coming together in preparation for winter when they must hunt in packs to survive. They find each other by howling. I had a sudden yen for wolf song, and soon said goodbye to Magnum Blatt and the Sand Hills and started driving north.

I had already found my way to Ely, Minnesota, which is way up north in the Boundary Waters shared by the U.S. and Canada. I had been there before because the International Wolf Center is there. They have a very handsome captive pack. I had raised a little money for them at my gallery in NYC by putting on an art show to celebrate the forest and its inhabitants. In addition to art, I showed films about wolves and I taught people to howl. Howling really does raise your energy. I was thrilled when asked by the Wolf Center in Ely to add my howl, (accompanied by imagined green twinkles) to a promotional tape.

I had already found a cabin in the area by simply following a sign that said "Wolf Lake." I believed the mother wolf who had appeared to me in New York was often by my side, guiding me in the right direction. And I didn't have to join a club to stay in this cabin overlooking a lake, just give a couple of days' notice. The owners were especially nice and I always felt welcomed.

It was brisk and bright and beautiful up there on the Boundary Waters. I loved the loons that lived on the lake and relished their long haunting calls. I watched a muskrat on his rounds in the lake each night, and saw beavers and otters at play. Unfortunately, I mentioned the otters to a local person whose face lit up with greed. I knew they might be trapped because of my enthusing big mouth! That was the last time I ever said anything about what animals I have had the good fortune to see. There are too many hunters and trappers lurking about!

Each night I kept alert for the sound of wolves. The third night, a voice commanded me to "wake up!" I jumped out of bed, heard nothing, then looked out the window to see a glorious display of northern lights moving over the sky. Well, of course, I said "thank you" to whatever spirit it was that awakened me.

The following night I had a clear vision of a dirt road and interpreted it to mean, "Go further out into the wilderness." So the next night I did. I parked in a deserted campground and sunk into my sleeping bag. Soon I heard voices, human voices. I was scared. I peeked out the window and saw four people and a big black bear. Wow, thoughts of bears had not entered my mind! I opened the window a bit and said, "Is that bear a friend of yours?" They all jumped about a foot off the ground and someone said, "Oh my god, there's someone in there!" Then in loud whispers they said they were from Earthwatch and they were tracking Jerry. Tracking Jerry? "Come on out and join us," they called, and I did just that. By the time I threw on some clothes and located my flashlight they had disappeared into the forest, but I could hear them and stumbled into the direction of their voices. Suddenly, I was charged by a bear. I had no way of knowing if it was Jerry, who seemed accustomed to human company, or some other bear who wanted to join in. I froze, hands at my sides. This bear licked both of my hands and threw itself on its back, paws in the air like a dog inviting a tummy scratch. I couldn't resist. I reached over and with one hand, pressed her paw and with the other, felt her very soft ear.

It seems the Earthwatch project was to observe the pre-hibernation behavior of this adolescent bear. To me, Jerry was the beautiful manifestation of the Bear Spirit who appeared to me in trance. I now believed the "Bear Itinerary" was complete. Astonishingly so! My hands will always remember the feel of her tongue and the soft fur of her ear. I wanted to make a button that read "Kissed by a Bear." I hadn't been kissed by anything else lately.

Later someone told me that Jerry just wanted to play but playing with adolescent bears is a bit dangerous unless you also have sharp teeth and claws. Until meeting Jerry, I had never seen a bear in the wild. Afterward, bears often ran across my path, dodging into bushes, disappearing into the forest, or just sauntered by. Later, on a hike in the Boundary Waters, I asked a forest ranger if any bears had been reported. "Nope," he said. "You could put a steak in your pack and be perfectly safe!" Twenty minutes later, a bear dove into the brush in front of me. I had the feeling then that I would be meeting them from now on. I was utterly charmed by them. And very respectful, of course!

Storytelling And Bears

In 1995 I was part of an Earth Day celebration at the Summer Song Gallery in Seattle. A circle of stones I'd painted with creatures of the sea was on display. There was a video in which I talked about my circles and I gave a story-telling performance I'd written called "How On Earth I Found a Voice." Earth Woman was in her green glory.

This time I had rented a van in Seattle and at the end of a long visit and excursions with friends drove onto the ferry for Vancouver Island. It was May. The lilacs were just blooming and bears were just leaving their winter dens. Bears seem to be a bit disoriented and groggy then, intent on foraging for food after their long nap. I saw quite a few as I drove and they didn't even look up as I passed.

I drove to Tofino on the coast. At a campground there I was warned never to hike alone because of hungry mountain lions descending from the mountains.

Having been on the road quite a lot, I was surprised there was no road kill, until I realized that what passed for forests there were really tree farms. And tree farms do not provide the environment necessary for nurturing such small animals as rabbits, skunks, and raccoons. No wonder the mountain lions were coming into town for a meal! It was such a problem at that time kids were not allowed to walk to school unaccompanied. Thankfully I did not bump into one.

But I did meet some very special people, several of whom were members of the Nuu-Chah-nulth tribe. They invited me to a ceremony on a nearby island called Wickanninish. I had some nice rocks in the van, so I painted a group for a small circle to add to the occasion. Smiling Indian women helped me load them on the boat and it was then I learned the ceremony was for bears. Bears killed by a Seattle football team. The team had come to Vancouver Island for a short holiday and each member left with a bearskin. We sang and prayed for those bears and those men. The drum we used was made from a beheaded bear thrown in a dump. Here's a poem I wrote about it:

Someone killed that bear
The bear you saw
Is a drum now
Its footprints are no more
Pressed into the earth
But painted walk
Across its skin
Its heart no longer pounds
With the beautiful blood that binds
But is a pulse now
On the wind
Played by those who love it
Who call it brother and grandfather
Spotted eagle cries
Swoops low
Feathers drift
Into our hands
We tie them
To that drum
Heads thrown back
Crying to the stars
We sing
Eagle Bear, Eagle Bear
You are going home
Going home now
Eagle Bear
You are home.

Tofino is on Clayoquot Sound. This Sound is full of lushly beautiful islands, many covered by old temperate rainforest. Not long after the Harmonic Convergence there were strenuous protests against cutting these forests. I met some of the brave people involved. I say brave because it was the policy of the government to put one or two random protestors in prison for a lengthy term as an example to the others. Both the lumber company and government were pretty ruthless. But the protestors, though sacrificing a lot, won. I kayaked among these islands and felt great gratitude to these people for the preservation of such profound beauty. I surprised my guides and myself by the passionate songs I sang for these islands and their huge ancestral trees, too big for hugging!

One of the early visions that came to me was about trees. In it, an old, heavily barked tree stood before me and became animated. It was trying to tell me something, but I could not hear it. Behind it stood some other trees but they were smooth and honey beige in color. I had seen trees like this in Vieques. Suddenly the trunks of the two closest ones opened and a man stepped out of one and a woman emerged from the other. What,

I wondered, could this possibly be about! Then I did find out, at least a little bit. The following week on a Tuesday when the *New York Times* always published its "Science Times" section there was an article relating that hemoglobin, a part of blood, had been discovered in the roots of some trees, "suggesting that trees and humans have a common ancestor." I often returned to this article over the following years but there was no evidence of further research for a long time. Now it is known that trees, humans, and plants are indeed genetically linked. It's no wonder many people like to hug trees and talk to their plants. Again, I thought about the stars connected by threads of light I'd seen on Bear Butte and felt that my comprehension of the interrelatedness of all life was being expanded by this vision of humans emerging from trees.

In Tofino I dreamt,"Trees are the antennae of the Earth." If so, then what are they sending? What are they receiving? One of the former demonstrators had a small boat to take tourists around these very inviting islands. He offered to take me with a friend of his to an island with hot springs. On the way we met up with a couple of gray whales, so of course I had to sing for them. The songs of whales are among the music I love most but not possible to hear on a boat. For me it is almost always a pleasure to meet a member of another species though I am unlike a friend in California who claims to have actually dated outside her species.

Our destination was an uninhabited island with a dock. There was a hike through forest that became a boardwalk over marshy land and ended at some big boulders. There we discreetly changed into our bathing suits for a hoped for submersion in hot springs. I froze in my tracks when on the other side of the boulders I saw a group of very naked young men lounging blissfully in the bubbling springs. Yipes! I gathered my cool and descended into the water among them and introduced myself. I mentioned I had just come from another island where there had been a ceremony for bears. They were interested because they were on a bear biology project from a university. We all relaxed. We talked bears. I told them about meeting Jerry. They knew the name of the bear biologist on that Earthwatch project. I learned from them the largest black bears in the world were north on the Queen Charlotte Islands where I was headed and that it was sometimes possible to take a ferry to Kodiak Island in Alaska, home to the largest species of Grizzly. My brother and I grew up with a Kodiak bearskin rug our grandfather bought in an auction just to get it out of the way. He was impatient to bid on some antique French fans. I briefly considered going out to Kodiak to see the rug we played in, come to life.

Every so often when it got too hot in the springs we would climb over boulders that bordered the ocean where you could perch and cool off when cold salty waves broke over them. After an afternoon of pleasant conversation and weaving back and forth from hot springs to cool waves, we all parted as friends and as allies of the "bear nation." (No pun intended here.) This coincidence added fruitfully to our communal interest in bears. The fact that most of us were "bare" made Earth Woman imagine doing gleeful "high fives" with that ingenious trickster/punster, Coyote. Coincidence happens so often but how does it occur? What makes it happen?

I continued driving north through Vancouver Island until I came to Strathcona Park. It was in the boundary areas of this enormous park that the bears had been taken by that football team. I camped in the park where snow was still melting and I made a commemorative prayer stick for the bears while being dive-bombed by newly arriving hummingbirds claiming their territories. Those tiny things are dangerously aggressive. There are many types of "prayer sticks" but the ones I make are standing forked branches that suggest a person standing with arms upraised in prayer. Sometimes I paint the stick or wrap it in ribbon or cloth and then attach feathers and tobacco prayer ties.

North By Ferry To Haida Gwaii

I had a reservation for Vanita von Van and myself on the ferry from Port Hardy at the end of Vancouver Island to Prince Rupert further up the coast of British Columbia. My cabin was simple but perfect. The food on board was good. The mountain scenery adorned by mists, the play of light, shadow, and moonlight was thoroughly absorbing. I could hardly believe my good fortune. Who needed anything more? But then a tall, very handsome Native man decided to pursue me. I can remember how he stood looking down at me, smiling, an invitation in his eyes and the seductive tone of his voice when he said, "I'm easy." I felt weak in the knees, scooted back to my cabin and locked the door. Romance was definitely no longer a part of my life!

My ultimate destination was Skidegate in the Queen Charlotte Islands. These islands, belonging to the Haida, are now known by their proper name, Haida Gwaii. It was a longer ferry ride from Prince Rupert than I imagined so I was glad I had booked a room for the night at a B&B. The streets were dark and deserted when I drove off the ferry, but when I located the house where I was to stay, there was no one there. There were no cell phones then, so I couldn't track down the owner but it didn't matter, I was accustomed to sleeping in a van now. It seemed as natural as sleeping in my New York apartment.

In the morning the owner was very apologetic, even more so because her extra room was full for the next few days so I got the locations of campgrounds from her and went into a café for coffee. It was clear that most people in the café knew each other well and I was a stranger. Very soon, however, they were gathering around to find out who and what I was and what I was doing there. I imagined visitors were not that frequent. I was adopted and I got invited to line dancing that night, something I had never tried before and quickly learned it isn't as effortless as it looks.

Quite a few of these people were descended from missionaries and had become teachers. I asked them about the bears and discovered how proud they were of their peaceful coexistence with them. Conflict was rare they said. They told me the Haida people and bears had lived together on these islands for 10,000 years and the Haida believed killing a bear was a crime. Mavis and Sergei from the cordial café group became my friends and mentors on the island. When I recounted to them how a mother bear with two cubs had passed near me without any indication they noticed me, how anxious I'd been and grateful they'd kept going, Mavis just laughed, "To those bears you were just another boring ho-hum human." That was fine with me but I would never regard a bear as another ho-hum bear!

It's hard to describe the beauty of Haida Gwaii's islands so abundant in lakes, old forest, beaches, hot springs, and snow-capped mountains. It seemed a magical land, fertile for the growth of myth and fable.

Mavis and others urged me to drive north to Agate Beach. It lived up to its name. The longer and closer I looked at its pebbles the more I could see the rich variety of patterns and colors, like tiny paintings on stone. I collected some of these stones to be used in a Native American "give-away" ceremony in New York. I painted a rock circle while camping there in my van. It was still May, very brisk and crystal clear. One of the café crowd had asked me when he heard I was from NYC, "How does it feel to breathe air you can't see?" It was especially cold out there on the beach. I slept with an extra blanket on top of my sleeping bag between the rocks I'd collected on Vancouver Island. I had a tiny canned heat stove and would emerge each morning just far enough from my cocoon to light it and heat enough water for coffee and a quick warm wash of hands and face. Then, one, two, three I would burst into the cold air, get dressed "pdq," and take a walk on this beautiful place where I was the only person in sight. My heart was full of song and I let it all out. One day a pleasant couple appeared and said they lived nearby, that Mavis had called them. She wanted me to know that Sarah Davidson, the wife of the Haida chief, would like to meet me. Like many Haidas they lived further north out in Old Masset. These visitors were so happy with the rock circle I had nearly finished that I said I would make one for them and I did. Then I drove out to Old Masset where I was warmly greeted by Sarah Davidson. I told her about my story performance, "How on Earth I Found a Voice" and said that I would like to give it there. She agreed and arranged for me to tell my tale in the Longhouse bearing her name. My audience was ten attentive and responsive Haida women. At the end, one came to tell me, with an air of confession, that early one morning while walking on the beach she had seen how the land was woven with threads like a cloth. What a beautiful and arresting vision! Wonder shone from her eyes as she recounted it and there was regret in her voice when she said she'd seen it only once. I was honored she shared this vision with me. I believe many people see such things but are afraid to speak about it. Children, however, are not, at least not until some stern adult says disparagingly, "That's only your imagination." How can any problem in the world, great or small be solved without first imagining a solution is possible and then imagining how to solve it? If healthy imagination is encouraged, maybe we can outsmart our banal consumer cultures. At the moment of writing this I learned that the science teacher in my granddaughter Gwen's school gives higher grades for imaginative, original thinking. I can't wait to meet her.

While I was in Old Masset I painted a stone circle for the Longhouse and while I was at work was surprised to see Mavis drive up. She had exciting news. There were some extra berths on a friend's sailboat. Some tourists had cancelled, and he was offering passage for the cost of the journey. They were going south through the islands of Haida Gwaii to Ninstints, a very remote World Heritage site famous for its Haida totem poles. Did I want to sign up? I was stunned by this amazing opportunity and by the kindness of these new friends. Mavis had driven some sixty miles with this invitation. Of course I jumped at this chance for a once in a lifetime experience!

We visited a Haida family on one island. They showed me where their dead were "buried" up in a tree. I was so moved I wanted to sing and asked permission. They really appreciated the song. When I told them it came from the spirit of an eagle, they embraced me. Among Haidas you are either a member of the Eagle or Raven moiety. Maybe this family's totem was the eagle.

On another island the tide was out so we stopped to view the intertidal life. I thought of the woman who had seen the land as a weaving because this was like a thickly woven, highly colorful, deeply textured carpet, and it throbbed with life. We walked into it but were afraid to move for fear of disturbing its intertwined multitude, a wonder to behold.

On another island we climbed to hot springs. On another we saw where clear-cutting of old forest had halted at midnight, a moment before the law prohibiting clear cutting of these forests became effective and we saw where the huge old trees continued in all their glory. It was like a line separating desolation and the miracle of life. The ten of us on board held hands and stretched ourselves as far as possible in an effort to encircle one of these splendid remaining trees but failed because it was so large. Though we felt certain we shared a moment of happiness with it. In great contrast I remembered driving up a forested portion of the Oregon coast and having to pull over because the need to "sing" was so strong. What poured forth from my heart were terrible groaning sounds and heart wrenching moans. I had to cry. Further down the road I learned this forest was about to be clear-cut. Even the distant memory of those sounds is painful. I try to think that I may have helped the spirit of this place in giving voice to its anguish just as I believe my voice released the pain of "Mon Coeur" the eagle.

We hiked other islands before reaching Ninstints three days later. Ninstints is a vision of a lost world with its powerful totem poles standing like guardians at the edge of the forest. Though many are in an advanced state of decay and many have fallen, they are alive with spirit and stories it seems they want to tell us. There is a strong feeling of longing about the place. It is a sacred place. Before these journeys by van I understood "sacred" as a concept. By the time I reached these islands, it was something I felt in my heart and bones. And I felt it often.

I didn't know how I could pry myself away from these beautiful islands and the generosity and wonderful camaraderie I experienced there. But I finally got on the ferry to Prince Rupert. A Haida man on board began a conversation with me. Very casually he remarked that some of his people were special and quite unusual. I responded by commenting that I had seen many extraordinary artists among the Haida.

"No," he replied, "That is not what I mean. What I mean is, long ago one of us married a bear and that blood still runs in some of us." He looked at me in a way that made me believe he was one of them. It was like a last gift, of so very many, from these magical islands.

From Prince Rupert I took the ferry to Sitka with a stop in Ketchikan. In Sitka I visited a raptor rehabilitation center where I saw the skinned corpse of a bear donated to the disabled eagles. As I had once read, a skinned bear does indeed, look human, alarmingly so. I had to sing for its spirit. This time my song was not appreciated but seemed to frighten the zookeepers. The eagles, however, became very alert and feathers were ruffled.

Mother Bear
Mother Bear
Spring be abundant I pray
In winterkill feast
Songs of hive
Nest and cocoon
All that lives
And flowering grows
With hunters gone
Far far away
That sunlight may cast your shadow
That you and your children
May walk with breezes
Bending the grasses once more

Mother Bear
Mother Bear
Many have sung to you
This song was mine

More Bears And The Wolf Clan

From Prince Rupert I plunged into the stunning interior of British Columbia. One park was famous for its waterfalls. There I attended a lecture on how to use pepper spray on bears. Timing was all-important and I was sure I would only succeed in making the bear angrier so I just put bells on my pack to let any resident bears know I was in the neighborhood.

I was frightened only once and that was when I saw a wee baby bear standing in the middle of the trail with its arms outstretched. It looked like a living teddy bear and I wanted to rush to it because it seemed lost. I didn't see a mother bear but knowing they are fiercely protective of their young I quietly and slowly backed up the trail until I hoped I was out of sight. I reported the little bear cub because it seemed in distress. The owner of the cabin where I stayed said he would check on it because there was a rumor that a bear had been shot. In idle moments I like to imagine happy endings to this episode.

On a hike to a glacial lake, a large bear crossing the trail stopped a second for a look at me and then dashed on. I smiled. It felt like a "hello." I had seen so many bears since that day when Jerry licked my hands and had never seen one before then. I began to imagine the possibility of some kind of energy threads connecting members of a species. What kind of information would these energy threads convey to black bears? "Claire is an okay human? Check her out?" Certainly it is easy to believe in threadlike connections as psychic energy in flocks of birds, schools of fish, or herd animals. How does your cat know you are leaving on a trip even though you have done nothing overt to suggest it? That is an example of interspecies connection/communication. Why does someone you are thinking about call you? My imagination likes to wander these fascinating trails. It is a rich adventure!

On the road I passed a hitchhiker but something made me stop and wait for him. He was an Indian, a young man on his way home to his village Kit Wan Kool. He said he had been away for quite a while but said little else. It made me anxious to pick him up but I had to trust my inner voice. When we stopped at an interesting looking trading post on the way, the owner, a woman, had a conversation with him. Then she took me aside and quietly said she had never heard of his family. This is unusual in the tribal world. Clearly she was warning me.

I was worried and could see the young man looked uncertain but we continued on. When we reached Kit Wan Kool, a very small place, this young man was greeted politely and became suddenly very animated when he saw the longhouse where a totem pole was being carved and walked me over to it. It was a commemorative pole for the chief of the Wolf Clan. The tall cedar tree was laid out on stands and three men were carving on it. The aromas of cedar and sage filled the air. We talked. I asked permission to sing for the Wolf Clan and they were very pleased and gave me the gift of a large scrap from the pole where they would be working intermittently for "another month or more." I was so honored.

Then a woman there sold me a black felt hat with a red felt applique of a wolf's head in the stunning abstract northwest Indian style. I was truly rewarded for my trust and I was sad not to see that young man again before driving off. Without him I would not have gone to Kit Wan Kool and had the wonderful experience of seeing a legendary totem pole in progress or met up with the Wolf Clan.

Continuing the journey, I headed south to Seattle to reluctantly return my van to the rental company but happy to give my performance again by popular demand. This time a group of beautiful young lesbians was in the audience and they so enjoyed my story, they made me an "honorary lesbian" and gave me the gift of a necklace hung with rainbow rings, the symbol of their sisterhood.

Sitting Bull And The Last Sundance

He said, "I know light when I see it!" It was 1992 at the conclusion of the last of the four Sundances in Green Grass I attended. I stood outside the supermarket in Eagle Butte having just loaded up on supplies for the final feast, when a stranger walked up to me and asked me how to get to Green Grass. I looked around, noting that I was the only non-Indian present. Laughing I said, "What makes you think I know where Green Grass is?" and I got that surprising reply, "I know light when I see it." I stared at him a moment until I was able to say, "Well, I'm going there now. You can follow me."

I had no idea I was leading the Pipe of Sitting Bull into Green Grass, the home of the ancient White Buffalo Calf Pipe. It was an accidental honor that will always amaze me. Nor did I know this stranger was a representative of the Cody family, (of Wild Bill fame) who had held Sitting Bull's Pipe for many years and now wanted to return it. The return of this Pipe expressed confidence in Arvol Looking Horse and the Lakota people.

I'd had a vision of four Indian heads emerging from the earth with four buffalo standing in attendance. I understood this vision to be about the rebirth of the Indian people and it struck me that this was what was happening at the presentation of the Sitting Bull Pipe. All the Sundancers, their supporters, and friends and people of Green Grass assembled and formed a circle that included many men on horseback. As the Pipe was handed to Arvol Looking Horse all the horses stamped and whinnied, surprising everyone, especially their riders, and making many of us cry. It was a great and significant moment. As if to honor the occasion, the land was radiantly lush, fragrant and green. The drought of seven years was over. Here's a poem about what happens when it finally rains in South Dakota:

Grass
Short grass
Tall grass
Curly grass and straight
Sharp bladed

Serrated
Long legged
Red legged
Brown tasseled tickle grass
Nut flavored
Honey sweet
Blue green gold grass
Flow-er-ing grass
Feather fluffy
Orange flagged
Burr tufted sticky grass
Spiny- balled owie grass
Bunch teasel
Buffalo grass
Sway bounce and skipping grass
Run – ning grass
Yellow beaded grain headed
Bird hiding
Antelope bedding
Spider loving
Snake snuggling
Grass grass grass
Scratchy Itchy
Fuzzy
Soft
Ankle grabbing
Thigh tingling
Sweet smelling
Sneeze making
Life giving
Light making
Yes yes
GRASS!

This Sundance, the last of four was followed by a "Give Away" in which people who had helped facilitate these four ceremonies received gifts of blankets and other goods from the Looking Horse family. Vincent Black Feather, the presiding medicine man, received a very beautiful black quarter horse. So often in Green Grass it was easy to imagine I might have magically traveled into the 19th century.

During this last Sundance the stones I painted were covered with stars, the year before, only buffalo. During the first two Sundances I painted animals of the world. I loved seeing these four stone circles nestled together in the grasses across from the octagonal Pipe House. At the end of the last dance I slept beneath those gracious cottonwoods along the Little Moreau for the last time.

For a time after that, Green Grass became closed to outsiders. There were rumors of conflict within the Looking Horse family regarding the admission of outsiders. Feelings of hostility toward white people began flaring up during the second Sundance and were even expressed in the Sweat Lodges.

I brought Rosy, a longtime Pipe holder and student of Martin High Bear to a Pipe ceremony there but she was not admitted because she did not have a card to prove that she was Indian. She had one but didn't think she would need it. We were not even allowed down the road to view the Pipe House at a distance. I was heartbroken but Rosy just shook her head and said, "Gee, Claire, I don't get it 'cause you're so real Indian looking" and broke into laughter. She was really talking about herself, unmistakably an Indian! We stopped at the home of Marian Egna, an elderly lady who befriended me, and we took her and her family out for dinner at the Eagle Butte steak house and had a fine time. Marian made small traditional star quilts for my little granddaughters.

The Harmonic Convergence took place five years earlier, and while my life had grown unbelievably rich, I was going broke. I closed my alternative gallery, gave "my artists," and the mailing list to another arts enthusiast, rented my studio for extra income and eventually sold it. It was a difficult move but I felt I had no choice. After thirty-five years of being a painter of pictures, I now had to pursue my vision of a web of painted rock circles around the continent and beyond. I was on a journey, and knew I must remain faithful to it, whatever it was and wherever it took me. I trusted it, though simultaneously claimed my middle name could be "self- doubt."

Web Work

Traveling around, living in a van, I almost always felt that I was in the right place at the right time, surprisingly, since I'd never been to any of these places before and depended on intuition and spirit to guide me. On two memorable occasions, however, I lost my confidence and ended up sobbing in remote motel rooms wondering if I was just a crazy lost soul! What did I think I was doing? Who did I think I was? Why couldn't I stay in my lovely New York apartment, enjoy my friends, my city, and the arts instead of wandering heaven knows where? I longed for some reassurance. A hug would have been good. However kind guiding spirits may be, they don't "do" hug.

Here's a poem I wrote when feeling lost on the western edge of North Dakota.

The name of this somewhat humorous poem is:

Some Of You Might Like To Know

> *Will a spirit guide*
> *Find me*
> *In a little town in North Dakota*
> *Way out on the western badland edge*
> *Where one hundred and three*
> *Will be low for the day*
> *Where hot winds singe*
> *The tips and fringe*
> *Of everything*
> *Will a spirit guide*
> *Find me there?*
>
> *Will a spirit guide*
> *Find me*
> *In the dusty road café*
> *Where a spilled cup of black coffee*
> *Couldn't stain a white napkin?*
> *Where mounted heads stare*
> *While families eat daily fried specials?*
> *Would a spirit guide*
> *Sit beside me there?*

Will a spirit guide
Find me
In the town's wind-worn motel
Where rooms are forlorn
And linens are thin
Where the mattress vibrates to a quarter
Dropped in a meter slot
Next to the bed
Would a spirit guide
Check in with me there?

Oh yes
You bet
I won't forget
To say, "thank you!"

The first time I felt lost and scared I was trying to complete a series of stone circles down the center of the continent. It was an important part of my vision of a web of circles. I'd already painted one in North Dakota in the Turtle Mountains, in South Dakota in Green Grass, and there was one in the Sand Hills of Nebraska that I had to be sneaky about. I had painted a circle of birds and took them to the ranger at the National Forest, and he said, "they wouldn't fit in." The women of the Sand Hill Painters said, "Those guys aren't ready for a prayer circle yet, hon," (an understatement). So I carried those bird stones to a quiet tall grass part of the National Forest and sang them into place.

Then I needed to place a circle farther south in Kansas, so I left my buddy Magnum and my dear cabin on the Snake River to drive through the southern part of the Sand Hills toward the Platte River. I savored this part of the Sand Hills in which all the Loup (French for "wolf") Rivers ran, though the wolves were long gone and as usual I seldom saw another car on the road.

I slept in my van for a night in a State Park just over the state line in Kansas. I walked around the land there and the lake and I liked it but the place just didn't "speak" to me. It didn't feel like a location for one of my stone circles. Nowhere did. I ended up way down south in Medicine Lodge, Kansas where I pulled into a small motel and cried myself to sleep. In the morning the kindly expression of the woman manager, whose name was Billie, inspired me to tell her about my rock circles. She looked at my map of the area and pointed out some local roads she said went through beautiful country—maybe I would find a location there, she said. She was right about the country, a beautiful landscape of reddish purple hills dotted with cedars and yellow wildflowers.

I did not, however, see a spot for a circle until returning to Medicine Lodge in the late afternoon and spied a little dirt road going up a rise. Although the land was fenced in like all of Kansas is, and had a sign that said "Private Property," there was no gate so I decided to take a chance, drive in and arrange the rocks that were in my van already painted. I'd be in and out before anyone could notice and I didn't see anything except the usual cattle. It was a great location, a small promontory looking out over the prairie. I arranged the stones, planted the small stone from Bear Butte, and while singing a prayer to connect it to the energy of Bear Butte I heard a roar and a harsh, "Hey!" I turned around to confront an angry looking bullish man who leapt out of his pick-up leaving the door wide open, the motor running and was striding toward me fast. The license plate said, "MEAT."

In my meekest voice I said, "I'm sure you may find this hard to believe, sir, but I am an artist from New York City and I've been looking for a location for my painted rocks. Of course I'll remove them right away if you object. Oh yes, my name is Claire L. Dunphy." He was certainly surprised, but he did believe me and was in fact touched as I explained that the sea creatures I'd painted were to commemorate the ancient sea that had once been there. He introduced himself as, George Fritz. Later another citizen of Medicine Lodge informed me that I was lucky not to be an "SSS, Shoot, Shovel, and Shut up," because George, who had been having problems with cattle rustlers, probably thought I was a lookout for them! That would never have occurred to me. I thought cattle rustlers belonged only in old Westerns.

George may have been tough but he did appreciate my rock circle. When those stones were later stolen from his land, he offered a reward and had me interviewed by the local paper.

Billie, the sympathetic motel manager, later took me into her home. Frequent shrieks came from that house because her husband, Frank expressed his playful nature by planting fake limbs beneath sofas and tables. Visitors never knew when they might stumble across a "corpse!" I was thankful to be forewarned. But Frank was a great guy and took me around to some of the historical sites and beauty spots in the area. He thought I would be interested in seeing a herd of "black baldies," black cattle with white faces. For some reason I found them to be very touching and sang to them. They had been grazing peacefully and suddenly looked up and began racing toward me. Frank and I quickly dodged behind the gate to this pasture. What were they thinking? What was I thinking?

The town barber turned out to be the town historian and a wizard rock hound. As a rock painter I naturally found all rocks of interest and this man gave me some special fossils. At the end of the summer when I returned my van, I had a lot of "special" stones that I couldn't toss out so I packed up my favorites and took the box to UPS. When picking it up, the man at the counter nearly lost his balance. He said, "Whataya got in here, rocks?" "Well, er," I think I blushed.

Then I discovered Charlie Little Coyote, a Cheyenne chief, and his wife, Vicki lived in Medicine Lodge. I had met them at a ceremony on Bear Butte.

Medicine Lodge was a place with an interesting history. A peace treaty had been signed there in the late 1800's and a reenactment of the occasion occurred every two years. The river there, now dry, had once been full of healing springs and Epsom salts and was considered to be sacred. It was a place with an intertribal history. Later on I painted a circle of buffalos for the Peace Treaty Park and was treated so cordially by so many people in Medicine Lodge that I even imagined buying a little house there. I had arrived confused and depressed and was welcomed into a special world.

Clearly all the trouble I had in finding a place for my stone circle that "felt right" to me, led to the place that was absolutely right. It almost seemed it was waiting for me to arrive. I told myself I must become more trusting, more confident that I am being guided. Before leaving NYC that summer I had a dream in which I was told, "Your fears are like comic book characters!" Wish I could remember not to take them so seriously!

Leaving Medicine Lodge, I continued south into Oklahoma intent on painting a rock circle there. And I did, in Osage State Park. It was in Pawhuska, Oklahoma that I learned the Osage people had, in the past, adopted the spider as their totem. Many of the women once had spider tattoos on the backs of their left hands. There is a portrait of a matriarch in a museum there in which this tattoo is prominent. Unlike many tribes, they were successful in integrating with Europeans, but were eventually overrun. The spider, they said, spins her web and waits for her food to arrive. With Spider as their totem, the Osage waited and indeed oil was found on much of their land and many became wealthy. Spider medicine protected and rewarded them.

Because of my "web visions" I had become a friend of spiders and curious about their many talents, stories, and legends. Ironic, because spiders were what I most feared as a child and I shudder now remembering how gleefully I sucked them up with a vacuum! In one of my dreams there I was told, "The fate of the planet must be re-spun."

Just as I had visualized a string of my rock circles down the center of the country, I imagined a series of circles going up the west coast but didn't have a plan. It was the spring following the last Sundance and I had been ill with diverticulitis, looming thyroid problems and briefly hospitalized. Although thankfully living as usual in my apartment on 85th Street, I was anxious and depressed. Grey Bear came to New York to give a Pipe Ceremony. He is a small compact man with a huge spirit who always finds a reason for laughter and who always gives the impression that he is delighted to see you. Having him as a guest was the "good medicine" I needed.

I introduced him to my former brother-in-law, an eccentric Englishman living in D.C. at the time of Clinton's inauguration. They really hit it off and Grey Bear got into the Inaugural Ball where he met the new Secretary of the Interior. Gales of laughter came from Grey Bear when he recounted his time there.

During his visit in my home I expressed an interest in doing a traditional vision quest on Bear Butte. I thought it might help me with my health problems. He was enthusiastic and said he'd like to do that too.

A Man With Spider Medicine

After Grey Bear's departure we spoke by phone a number of times and in one conversation Grey Bear mentioned a medicine man named Galen Drapeau who had "spider medicine." My energy picked up right away. I hoped he might have insights into my web visions. "Does he have a phone number?" I asked.

I called Galen Drapeau and introduced myself—silence. I said I was a friend of Grey Bear—silence, that I had seen webs in visions—silence, that I wanted to do a vision quest on Bear Butte—pause, and then, "My house is just a couple of miles above the dam, it's yellow. You'll see it." Click!

I was on East 85th Street in Manhattan imagining that remote corner of South Dakota where he lived, what roads were there and hoped I could find the right house in the vastness of that land! I imagined I could have a consultation with Galen Drapeau before meeting Grey Bear at Bear Butte and if I felt I couldn't do the formal Vision Quest, I would just go to the mountain and support Grey Bear.

I rented a van as usual in the Minneapolis airport and after a visit with my friends there traveled into South Dakota toward Lake Andes. As I drove up the hill to what I hoped was the Drapeau house, I felt the anxiety which comes when you're making a big commitment but don't fully understand what the commitment is really all about. I don't think I was breathing when I knocked on the door. It was opened right away by a friendly-looking man who said, "I'm Galen." When I peeked inside I saw a large table with men seated all around it. I wanted to run, but Galen invited me to sit down and I made an attempt to explain myself. They all listened politely to the story of my visions and rock circles. Then Galen asked the men, "What do you see here?"

The man, who turned out to be a chief of the Choctaws, said, "I see someone who has helped a lot of people." And they all nodded and I felt embarrassed. Perhaps it's true but I never thought of myself in that context but more as someone who had received a lot of help.

Thankfully, Hope, Galen's wife, arrived with some of their kids so I was spared further commentary. We all hit it off right away and Hope and Galen invited me to park my van outside their house. I felt so welcome. Their children were a joy. Next day Galen took me to find some medicinal plants he needed, and I was included in a jaunt to the junkyard to search for a car door part.

Galen assured me that someone would give me a Pipe. You must have one for a traditional Vision Quest. Both he and Hope were certain that a medicine man would come to "put me up," the expression for being installed somewhere on the mountain for four days of fasting and prayer. Tradition demands that someone assist you with the requisite Sweat Lodge, both before and after your time "on the mountain," and in preparing the place of the Vision Quest and further instructions and interpretations.

They presented me with a beautiful star quilt, the traditional gift for the medicine man attending your vision quest and mentioned that I should have some gifts for that man's helpers. If Hope and Galen hadn't been so matter of fact, kind and reassuring while I expressed endless doubts, I'm sure I could not have undertaken the Hanbleyca, (Vision Quest).

Before leaving, I took them all to the supermarket and bought a load of good food. I didn't have enough cash so I drove ten miles to the tribal casino where I could use an ATM card. I knew Hope and Galen would give away a lot of what I'd bought because that is their way of life and that was fine with me.

I promised to paint a rock circle for them on my return because they really liked what I was doing. And so, with a full heart, I drove on to Sturgis to meet up with Grey Bear and do the traditional Vision Quest, Hanbleyca on Bear Butte—if I received a Pipe—if a medicine person was willing to "put me up." If, if, and if.

When I left Galen's home I planned to drive to Bear Butte through the Badlands. It was something I now looked forward to. On the lonesome road I passed a young Native woman on foot. A little further on I saw a dead doe. It spooked me and I turned around to offer that girl a ride. She was an unmarried mother, on her way to another reservation. She was touchingly polite and proud. I changed my route to get her near the interstate where she would have a better chance of getting a ride to her destination. Being on the road is sometimes about more than reaching your personal destination.

Imagine those often used expressions, "cast of thousands," "madhouse" manifested, put in a jar and shaken up and you would have an idea of what I found when I arrived at Bear Butte. That place I associated with peace and solitude was buzzing like a human beehive. I parked in the special parking lot, walked across the little wooden bridge that spans a small ravine and entered the area designated for camping and Sweat Lodges and froze at the sight of this sea of humanity. It was teeming with Native Americans putting up their tents, waiting for Sweat Lodges and making tobacco ties.

Word was that this many people, (estimated at 400-444) had not been on the mountain for one hundred years. After much deliberation Grey Bear and I had picked this date at the end of May for our vision quests and so apparently did a lot of other people, but why the crowd? I never did get a straight answer, but think the arrival of so many people was related to a powerful eclipse of the full moon that was said to bring awareness of the divisions and relationships between opposites such as the spiritual and the practical, the intuitive and the rational. Additionally, there was a partial eclipse of the sun preceding it by ten days. Although my knowledge of astrology is limited, I did understand this could be a fruitful period of time for the inspired visions and spiritual guidance, that all of us there hoped for.

When Grey Bear and I had agreed on this date we had no idea there would be a crowd. Where was he anyway? Would I be able to find him? I felt so disoriented. I scanned the crowd for a familiar face and spotted George, a rock "reader" in Sweat Lodge ceremonies whom I'd met in Green Grass. He said Grey Bear and his family were staying in the Cheyenne Lodge on the other side of the mountain and that the Cheyenne had been "putting up" a lot of people. Then Phelps, a Cheyenne medicine man, suddenly appeared and announced he had just "put up" a number of women and that the men were just "coming down" and I heard him say he'd be putting up Grey Bear. My head was spinning trying to grasp the idea of crowds, and the regimentation of groups being put up and coming down. I was put off! I wandered up the mountain looking for a quiet spot to think about all this only to meet paramedics descending with a woman who had broken her ankle. Anxious and tired from the drive from Galen's house on the other side of South Dakota and all the confusion, I retired to a motel in Sturgis for a quiet night after a meal at Bob's.

After a good night's sleep the situation began to look a little bit funny. All that careful planning landed us in chaos. All our seriousness and spiritual intensity was suddenly like so many whoopee cushions. It was one of those rare moments when you view yourself from a distance and just shake your head and laugh. The anticipated demonstration of opposing energies brought about by the eclipse seemed to be in full sway.

It felt as though coyote the trickster was on the prowl and that I, at least, would just have to roll with his punches. Believing I was ready to do so, I returned to the mountain where things seemed less frenzied, but was right away approached by an attractive Lakota man who said, "I'm looking for a traditional white woman with a credit card."

"Well," I laughed, "I guess you'll just have to keep on looking."

A small area defined by prayer flags was pointed out to me. "This is where a Heyoka is doing a Hanbleyca." At first I didn't get the significance of this. A Heyoka is a medicine man who has received the special transformative visions that lead him into the life of the Contrary or Sacred Clown. It's a hard life but an important role in Native American cultures. This Heyoka was not confined to the area defined by his prayer flags. He was wandering around the mountain. By doing the opposite of what tradition demanded, what was he teaching? Perhaps he was suggesting a vision could be received in other ways. If you were to ask him he would tell you the opposite of what he meant. The contrary actions of the Heyoka seem to say, "Think again. Take another look" or "Don't take yourself, (or the situation,) so seriously or give more serious attention." Or it could be the opposite. His sheer presence or lack of it seemed a manifestation of what was happening on the mountain. He brought a sacred teaching to the confusion on the slopes of Bear Butte.

Now it no longer seemed so daunting but possibly instructive and interesting instead. The Lunar Eclipse played its part. Coyote played his part but the Heyoka seemed to have the last take on the extraordinary occasion of so many people of different ages, and different tribes seeking Hanbleycas simultaneously on Bear Butte. He seemed to indicate, "This is life, it is full of opposites and contradictions. All of it is taking place on a sacred mountain. Learn!" What could the sacred mountain represent other than Earth herself?

Hanbleyca

hen at last I met up with Grey Bear and his sister Mona they were accompanied by her three children, her fiancée Lyle, and their little nephew Quentin, whom they had just rescued from family services while their sister Bertina received medical attention after being beaten up by her drunk husband. It seemed like a "cast of thousands" rerun! As soon as I caught my breath, they told me the Cheyenne lodge was closing and they had no place to stay. Part of every New Yorker's verbal repertoire is the Yiddish expression "Oy!" usually accompanied by hand on forehead and eyes rolled upward seeking divine intervention.

While hanging on to my insights into the Heyoka and Eclipse, and silently repeating "oy oy oy" I swept up the disheveled Grey Bear clan, took them to Bob's for food and my decent motel in Sturgis. And hoped that all the opposing energies would allow me to have a quiet night of rest. I should have known better. Before sunrise an upset Mona was at my door to tell me her brother and fiancée had insulted her. I gave her a little talk about how sometimes people try to manipulate each other and put her to bed. Then came a grumbling Lyle. To him I said they were all tired and not thinking straight. In a huff he marched off on foot to Bear Butte.

Grey Bear and I met for breakfast and I was relieved to learn that Phelps was not putting him up. I told him I wasn't prepared for all this confusion and being surrounded by needy people when I needed to prepare for the Hanbleyca, something for which I had no previous experience. He had just told me that Mona, Lyle, and children had nothing. They had no tents, no blankets, and no food. I decided to stop whining and take care of the situation. I bought tents and supplies. I put them up at the motel several more days because it became cold and rainy. The motel had laundry machines and that was a help to them. Their car was full of stuff but junked and broken and I was sure that would be the eventual fate of whatever I provided. It is the ambivalent, passive/aggressive way of many people on the reservations. It's a safe way to express anger but a sad waste of good energy.

Mona had not brought a quilt for Grey Bear to give to the attending medicine man so I gave him one, and although he said more than once that Mona would give me a Pipe, there was no mention of it. In the middle of these needy people I worried that my needs would not be met. But they were.

Grey Bear set up their tents near a Sweat Lodge being run by a young apprentice of Martin High Bear. His name was Nappy Ross. We gave him tobacco and he agreed to put us on the mountain. In the first sweat with Nappy I was greatly moved by his singing and the big spirit lights that danced around us. He was banned from the state of Minnesota for his activities with the American Indian Movement. I feel sure he was justified in whatever he did. He was a model of clarity and had a gift for listening better than anyone I knew. I was utterly enamored with his six-year-old son, Macoutz, (Bear Cub), who earnestly warned everyone to watch where they stepped to avoid hurting the ants. The exhortations of Macoutz have remained with me over the years.

Between caring for the Grey Bear family, which included finding clothes for that magical baby Quentin, and taking the other kids on hikes, Grey Bear and I each needed to make more than 600 prayer ties on a continuous string. Unconsciously we were fully engaged in the drama of opposites, the spiritual and practical demands of the situation. We were a perfect illustration of the interplay of these energies.

Prayer ties are tiny cloth bundles containing tobacco into which we breathed our prayers. The color of the cloth indicates to which direction the prayer is addressed. Once started, it's amazing how much you can find to pray for! We sat mumbling prayers for hours in the front seat of my van amid scraps of red, yellow, white, black, blue and green cloth and lengths of red string in a fog of smoke from the sage we burned. Mona said she would make my walutta—what was that? It's a piece of red felt with tobacco tied in the corner with red thread, an eagle plume and an abalone disk. It's for "Protection." Still, no mention of a Pipe and I didn't feel I could ask.

The Sweat Lodges were busy with people preparing for their time on the mountain. Our turn would come soon. We had the new clothes that must be worn before ascending the mountain, sleeping bags, quilts, the prayer ties, our prayer flags attached to long chokecherry branches. When we cut those branches from chokecherry bushes on the Cheyenne side of the mountain, a small breeze arrived as we gave thanks. Grey Bear said it was a spirit acknowledging our prayer. We needed large garbage bags to cover ourselves in case of cold or rain.

I still had not received a Pipe and at last Grey Bear asked his sister for it. She sent one of the children to the car to find it. The children started to say something about it but were shushed. Then Mona said, "It doesn't hold together well." It was a small woman's Pipe, and essential to a traditional Vision Quest, the Hanbleyca.

When at last our moment arrived, we took a final bite of food and drink of water and entered the Sweat where Nappy conducted the ceremony. He was "putting up," four people. It was a very unusual Sweat. Every rock that was brought in burst into flame. George, the rock reader, was visibly agitated. A stripe through the center of one stone glowed during the entire ceremony, reminding me of the division and struggle of opposites.

By the time our Sweat Lodge ceremony ended, it was dark. We stumbled out into the chilly night clutching our kinnickinnick (tobacco and red willow bark) loaded Pipes. Dizzy and disoriented from the heat and steam, we changed into our new clothes behind the lodge, not speaking a word. Holding our Pipes before us we slowly we made our way up to Grey Bear's chosen spot on the beautiful saddle in the mountain facing north. Speaking to anyone other than the medicine man is not allowed so I couldn't say anything to him, but we exchanged a quick glance of encouragement.

We continued our slow careful ascent of the mountain with Nappy and his fifteen-year-old Canadian assistant, Pete. Another person was helped into his Vision Quest spot and that left me and one other person still to be placed. As the climb became steeper I suddenly saw that the bowl of my Pipe was missing. It was gone. It had, I supposed, fallen somewhere. My heart fell. I thought I was holding the Pipe firmly. Then Mona's words registered, "It doesn't hold together well." Crying, I told Nappy that I had lost the bowl of my Pipe, that it fell somewhere on the trail. Nappy looked at me for a long moment, didn't speak, just nodded and went down the path with Pete. I was trying not to feel desolate. The remaining seeker of visions, a man, didn't help when he said, in haughty tones, "Well, that's the end of your vision quest." I could say nothing. I feared he was right. He had given a lengthy speech in the Sweat while Grey Bear and I confined our feelings to modest thanks.

But somehow Nappy found this small red stone pipe bowl, still filled and handed it to me after gently showing me how to wrap the Pipe and attach the bowl with a sage leaf after licking it. He told me not to worry, that he would give all the necessary prayers. Moments later when I looked into the bowl of the Pipe I had a dizzy spell. I stumbled, and almost fell. I saw the bowl was swirling with life, trees, mountains, animals, rivers. It spun and all became a blurred rainbow light. I couldn't speak, just kept climbing the trail with tears of gratitude streaming down my face until I got to my beloved "perch" looking east. Nappy installed my prayer flags and wound the string of 600 prayer ties around them, sectioning off my place, a square on the rocky earth, for meditation and prayer. My Pipe was placed before me. I was wrapped in the star quilt from Galen and Hope that I later gave to Nappy. I sang and Nappy sang.

I prayed until sunrise so happy to be in this, my favorite place near the top of Bear Butte. It felt like home. I had a strong sensation that I was at the tip of a sunbeam and I could feel the pulse of it. The birds flying around left little trails of red light making a net that seemed a manifestation of the web/membrane spoken of by that voice my first night on Bear Butte five years before. I smelled tobacco so I knew a spirit was keeping me company. I was in an ineffable state of wonder so it took a while to understand that I'd already received my vision. That the vision I sought was given to me on the trail! That it occurred when the bowl of the Pipe was recovered and reattached to the stem and I saw that all of life swirled within it. It gave me worlds to think about the two nights I spent on the mountain and still does. Now I knew the true meaning of praying with this Pipe that was now in my care.

On the afternoon of the second day a group of six "black eagles" (turkey vultures) flew straight down the mountain, so close to my head the rush of their wings rippled through my hair. I knew then, reluctantly, it was time for me to go down the mountain. When I arrived at the special campground, Nappy was there. He said the Sweat was ready, that

"We saw them," referring to the black eagles, and added that I must not speak until after the ceremony in which I would I smoke my Pipe for the first time.

Later Nappy told me he had found a spider on my white prayer flag, the color for the south. This meant that a healing was needed, and the black eagles indicated that a cleansing was taking place. They and their vulture kin are among the great cleanup crews of the planet! He also confided that I had picked the hardest possible time for a vision quest, so many polarities. When I came out of the Sweat, my dear friend Joanie from Blackhawk was waiting outside. How did she know? "Just had a feeling," she said.

With a little grin Nappy told me the man who claimed my vision quest was "over" didn't last the first night. Ha! Grey Bear stayed three nights. He had terrible dreams of drugs and alcohol and a yellow taxi out of control and dropping his Pipe. Nappy explained the dreams demonstrated what could occur without the Pipe and said again it was a time of opposing energies. Well, we picked it!

Nappy told us Martin High Bear was running a Sundance in Medford, Oregon, and maybe I could come along for a healing. I was more than ready. "I'll finally meet that great man, Martin High Bear." I exclaimed.

"Oh he's my uncle," Grey Bear remarked casually.

"Really!?" was my dumbfounded response. I was a bit outraged that I hadn't known this before and couldn't say a word. Martin High Bear seemed almost mythical to me since the mention of his name, six years before, had led me to Bear Butte for the first time.

High Bear Sundance

After a few more meals with family and friends at Bob's Restaurant, Grey Bear and I stopped at the Sioux Trading Post in Rapid where someone who knew Scott Lupi in Kyle said he'd been on a binge. My heart sank remembering that nice young man who had given me my second eagle feather. I hoped he would be all right.

A storm was brewing. There were flood warnings. So after picking bundles of tall sage near Sturgis we drove off to Spearfish to visit Ted Wolf and his family. They greeted us warmly. It seemed Grey Bear knew just about everyone you'd like to meet. Ted Wolf makes copies of old Indian beadwork for places like The Smithsonian. His moccasins were beautiful enough to make you weep. Grey Bear and I continued to Devil's Tower, where the "tower" which had always looked like a giant crystal to me, now seemed more like an immense tree trunk.

We then drove to Ten Sleep, Wyoming where the figures in old rock paintings looked like E.T.s to me, and Sun Dancers to Grey Bear. Maybe we were both right! Then we went to the hot springs in Thermopylae where we soaked in medicinal waters. We wandered through Yellowstone, and on to the stunning volcanic landscapes of Craters of the Moon National Park, in Idaho. We were headed toward Boise because my older daughter's exuberant mother-in-law lived there and I wanted to stop and say hello.

We were cruising along when Grey Bear gave a shout. He'd just seen a dead owl by the side of the road. I stopped, backed up, Grey Bear reached for my sweater, the nearest cloth available for picking up dead owls, and hopped out of the car. "But that's my GOOD sweater" I silently protested. There was the owl, encased in my turquoise chenille sweater in the back seat. Also had to make a screeching stop when Grey Bear spotted a beaver by the road. Thankfully it was a piece of carpet.

On entering Boise, I decided the van looked a disgrace and stopped at one of those fancy car washes where you can sip cappuccino and watch your precious vehicle through picture windows as it experiences a sort of spa treatment for cars. A man in a suit appeared.

He apologized, "I'm so sorry we have to keep your van." I thought "Oh no, the owl, it's illegal," but then he continued, "It just didn't get clean enough the first time through." I smiled brightly. At least mud and dust aren't against the law.

After some hard driving we got to the Sundance outside Medford, Oregon the next night. I crept to the back of the van to sleep and could hear the murmurings of a number of men, all expressing concern over the owl. They at last agreed it was unlucky for the Sundance and it was taken up into the mountains and left in a tree to dry. I later heard someone got a beautiful owl feather fan. My sweater did recover its luster but every time I wore it I had the sensation I was sharing it with an owl. Not a bad feeling.

With Martin High Bear I felt like Dorothy meeting the Great and Powerful Oz. He was a small and highly charged whirlwind of a man. Once during the four days of the Sundance I saw Nappy whisper something to him and nod in my direction. Martin looked straight at me and his face, for an instant, appeared enlarged. A few moments later he said into the microphone "That woman from New York just got the healing she wanted."

I painted a rock circle for him. Maybe I seemed a bit hesitant when I brought the stones to the door of his trailer, because he said, "Don't you worry, I'll take good care of them. One of my names is Rocky Boy, you know." And he added with a smile that I could call him "Uncle Martin." I was enamored! There was always a circle of chairs in front of his trailer. You could sit there whether he was physically present or not, though the presence of his energy could always be felt.

I'll never forget the sound of Martin's voice as he said to the assemblage, "The Creator, He loves you no matter what you do!" He also said that happiness is God's greatest gift to us and that we should try to feel it, be happy.

It was in a Sweat Lodge held during this Sundance that I saw the spirit of the African Fishing Eagle who tore open my heart and pulled a song from it. I knew then he must be dead and his spirit was with me. It still is. It was a woman who ran that Sweat and she later suggested I speak to the eagle I had already named, Mon Coeur in French. In another Sweat the medicine man said that I would receive a healing for the pain in my shoulder. I wondered how he knew about it. Later while taking a nap I felt tapped on the shoulder and the pain left. I met the granddaughter of Mad Bear Jackson, a famous Tuscarora medicine man. When I told her about Jerry the bear licking my hands, she told me I might be blessed with healing energy in my hands.

This Sundance was much more friendly than the one in Green Grass. These people were accustomed to seeing outsiders. In fact, it was a beautiful mixture of people from different tribes, races, and places. Love was in the air. Maybe that was partly due to the size of the Moon Lodge where thirty women were housed. Their collective prayers were seen as positive loving energy supporting the dancers.

Men were pierced and pulled away continuously over the four days and people felt free to enter the ring and dance behind them to give support. On the final day when healing was given, the children danced and the Sundancers brushed us with their eagle feathers and eagle feather fans. The earth itself seemed to pulse with love. How grand it was!

Galen, a man of many aspects, also ran Sundances. In one I attended he appeared in his Heyoka persona. He wore army fatigues, a green beret, had a big cigar dangling from his lips and as he approached the dancers who were already pierced, he reached down to adjust his balls. He played the ultimate macho. He made a good joke of it. I could see the dancers appreciated this parody and that their participation in the Sundance had nothing to do with proving their masculinity. I brought my sister-in-law, Jane, to another Sundance hosted by Galen. When we arrived he came forward with his Pipe and announced that he was inviting us to smoke it. This surprised many of the Native people there but Galen, as a dedicated teacher of tolerance, didn't hesitate to demonstrate it.

After so many Sundance experiences I had to ponder the meanings of suffering and sacrifice in a different way. It seemed to me their glorification had created a lot of hell on earth. Though it is a normal part of life to sometimes suffer and sacrifice for what we love or believe, the ritual of it signifies something more, the powerful intention to intervene, to change the course of something, which can range from an individual's threatened health to tribal or national well-being. I believe the gods are moved by such clear pure intent.

As the High Bear Sundance came to an end, I felt so bereft I rented a room in the

Medford Motel 6 so I could cry in private—sob, really. The profound and beautiful experiences of the Hanbleyca followed by the Sundance were concluding.

I returned to the Sundance encampment next morning explaining humorously that I couldn't adjust to flush toilets and had to return for the outhouses. The truth, of course, was different. I would now suddenly be alone after so much rich experience with so many special people and all the care and affection we had exchanged.

And I had begun to deeply understand that healing takes place when the heart is able to welcome the love that is everywhere. During one of the many Sweat Lodges that took place during the High Bear Sundance, I saw a stag enter the lodge. He said, "My heart is your heart. Your heart is my heart."

Rocking Up The West Coast

Grey Bear drove south with his old friends from California, and I was once again alone to pursue my vision of a web of painted stone circles connected to Bear Butte. I drove down into Northern California to walk among the magnificent Redwoods. In a park nearby I began painting some stones. A ranger spotted them, "I don't know if that's legal." Another said, "That could be defacement." I got out of there fast and shot back to Oregon, this time to Gold Beach. There I found a cabin where my soul was soothed by the music of the rolling surf and I intended to stay a while to drink it in.

Many mornings on this beach, a ribbon of mist hovered along the water's edge. I would step into it and everything would disappear. Then I would jump out the other side where the world would brilliantly reappear like a magician's scarf trick. Or I could jog along the edge of the mist and see everything as through a smoky lens. I was recovering from those intense ceremonies and in a playful mood. One of those mornings I sat in the sand to watch this mist glowing and undulating like a living thing that might have come from the sea. While I watched, a melody emerged from its depths, a dreamy melody that wrapped itself around me like a soft, comforting blanket. I heard the melody again in a dream that night with the words, "wani a lo." Later I expanded it into a song that's in my CD for children called "Why I Love Life So."

I opened the door to my cabin one afternoon and froze in my tracks. There was rainbow lying across the bed, a spooky, alien rainbow. I could not see where it was coming from. At last I saw that a beam of sunlight had entered a high narrow window at the rear of the cabin, hit the beveled edge of a mirror, refracted and shot across the room to lie as a rainbow across the bed. Now that I understood it, it seemed a friendly invitation.

I put my hands in it and watched the colors glide over my fingers. I lay on the bed so that it could run the length of my body and best of all put my head in it at different angles so I could visually experience one color at a time—just red, just yellow. Blue was the most intense. In a dream that night I saw a rainbow fly in through the window and I heard a whisper as it circled my throat. When I reached up to touch it, I felt feathers and saw they were the colors of the rainbow but powerfully iridescent and they hung from a thread of golden light. When the sun rose it flew back through the window the way it had come. I don't think I've had such beautiful dreams again as I had at Gold Beach.

I still had the apparently illegal rocks I'd begun to paint in California, found some more and painted two circles that were very appreciated by both guests and owners of the cabins in Gold Beach.

A week or so later, continuing this coastal journey, I got a late start and I was worried about finding a place to pull in for the night. Thankfully I didn't miss a small sign at a bend in the road that simply said, "campground." It was a little spot with ten cozy campsites separated by tall, well-pruned hedges. At first glance there was nothing to suggest the wonders that were in store.

Wandering around in the morning I came across a trail that climbed through lush temperate rainforest full of ferns and thick mosses. It led to a sudden view of the stunning Sahara-like sand dunes of the Oregon coast and then plunged down into the dunes. I was taken by surprise. I knew about the dunes but had no idea I would be seeing them here unannounced.

I teetered there anxiously until an osprey swept down, nearly touching my head. Reassured by the presence of this fishing eagle, I continued down the trail through the towering dunes into a scrub forest with its bogs and lichens until I burst out onto a wide beach alive with birds. The heads of curious seals popped up in the ocean and there wasn't another human soul present. On another day I decided to surprise the watching seals by doing cartwheels along the beach but when I stood up they had all disappeared. None were flapping their flippers in applause.

It seemed a paradise to me and of course I wanted it to be a location in the series of stone circles I hoped to continue painting on the west coast. I had lovely river rocks in the van and I started painting. The campground manager took an interest in what I was doing and eventually said that if I cared to leave a circle there, she would look after it. How fortunate and blessed I felt and still do.

A week later as I prepared to leave, she presented me with a lively translucent yellow agate and said, "My mother loved stones. I found this one in her pocket when she died and I want you to have it." Her mother was buried in Ketchikan and she hoped if I got there I would I leave a stone on her grave. Of course, I promised. The following year I was on a ferry going to Sitka after painting rock circles on Vancouver Island and on the Queen Charlotte Islands. The ferry stopped in Ketchikan where in a heavy rainstorm I was charmed by the sight of trees full of bald eagles, not pigeons. There was one taxi and the driver, Harry, drove me to the cemetery carrying a stone I'd painted with a hummingbird. Neither Harry nor I could find the grave but he promised to bring it to the cemetery manager the following day. Five days later, on the return trip from Sitka there was only a short stop in Ketchikan, not long enough for me to disembark but "Harry the Good" was there giving me the thumbs up sign, mission accomplished! I was so happy. We are connected to one another, through time and space in such beautiful and surprising ways. So it seems.

Painting stone circles on the West Coast carried me north to the lush rainforests of the Olympic Peninsula where I felt I was hiking in scenes from a magical fairytale that included the exotic, (to me) banana slug. Then I reached La Push on the Quileute reservation. Here was another tribe I'd never heard of. I was embarrassed by my ignorance of tribal names and histories. Why has American education overlooked the complex and rich tribal history of this continent?

The small hotel at La Push was full but the people in charge allowed me to park on the grounds and live undisturbed in my van. It rained, usually lightly, nearly all day every day. I was amused that no one seemed to notice. Everyone went about their lives as though the sun shone, without umbrellas or raincoats. They were, so to speak, perfectly attuned to their environment. I started painting rocks and once again, because people were so welcoming, I kept on painting and was invited by that hotel to leave the circle there. At a small ceremony for the circle I gave away tee shirts that were printed with some of the images of my animal cutouts. Joe Geshick had begun to print some of his images on tee shirts and he and Sara encouraged and helped me to join in. There was "Bear Dance," "Love Dove," and "Wolf Song." A "Giveaway" is often a part of Native American ceremonies. Gifts are given to express gratitude and I was grateful indeed that my health had improved, for my wonderful vision on the Hanbleyca, for the kindness and generosity of so many people, AND that I could address Martin High Bear as "Uncle Martin!" I felt special.

Someone at the celebration for this stone circle said, "Oh, you must go to Neah Bay and meet Isabel Ides. She's a great storyteller."

"Where does she live?" I asked, hoping as always for clear directions in places unknown.

The reply was, "Somebody there can tell you how to find her." As abbreviated as this information was, it was a lead to the next part of my journey in which I depended on "leads" to find my way and fulfill my vision. I was relieved because I really didn't have a clue at that point where to go next and felt somewhat bewildered in the imposing wilds of the Olympic peninsula.

It was a long and lonely drive to Neah Bay and I arrived late at night in a dense fog. The place reeked of dead fish. The motel was dreary and dispiriting, clearly a place for fishermen to fall into. The whole place oozed depression. I cried myself to sleep, once again moaning, "Why, why do I have to be like this? What am I doing and where am I anyway? Why can't I settle down and enjoy my life in NYC?" I rarely felt discouraged but when I did my determination to continue manifesting my vision of a web of painted stone circles connected to Bear Butte did not falter.

In the gloomy morning I approached the local café with a feeling of dread. The waitress was a young Indian woman wearing a necklace of "hickies," dark bruises around her neck—was this in lieu of an engagement ring I wondered, a local custom perhaps? She smiled, and saying nothing, handed me a menu that was like a travel brochure. It informed me that I was in Neah Bay, the farthest point west in the continental United States and the home of the Makah tribe. I perked up a bit and asked the waitress if she knew where Isabel Ides lived. "I heard a her," she replied, while clearing something from the table, then returned to say, "Better go down the road an' ask someone out there."

Isabel Ides And The Green Flash

It was good to drive away from the intense reek of fish. I stopped someone in the road who just said, "Isabel? She's out that way." I kept going, didn't see a thing, took a left until the forest started closing in. I figured I should have taken a right and turned back. The optimism I'd managed to muster was slipping away and I was about ready to forget the whole thing. But when I returned and took the right fork, within moments a handsome bald eagle swooped down, brushing the hood of my van and I knew I was in the right place at the right time.

I was excited and laughed remembering what Yogi Berra, the famous baseball player purportedly said, "When you come to a fork in the road, take it!" The gloom lifted and the road opened up to beautiful coastline. I could see a whale spouting on the horizon. Soon I came to a small wooden house with a totem pole in front and knew that must be it. I parked in the road, opened the gate, climbed a few steps to the front door and knocked three times. When the door was opened by a pleasant looking gray haired lady, I said, "Isabel Ides?" She peered at me and said, "Give me a moment. I need to put my teeth in." I smiled and said, "I really need to get my glasses from the car."

Isabel invited me in. As soon as we sat down she told me her husband had died not long before and that during his final illness she was awakened every night by three knocks on the door. It frightened her but her husband told her not to be afraid. I was amazed that Isabel would tell me something so intimate without any preamble! Was it my three knocks? I thought for a moment and then said I thought the knocking was to tell her that many people would be visiting her because she carried many tribal stories, and spoke the language of the Makahs. "You are important, Isabel," I said. "Some Quileute people sent me to you and I think many people will be sent to you now."

I didn't know then that she was a very famous basket maker. She invited me to camp on her land but then sent me to her nephew's campground because it had toilets, but she warned me that he wasn't a very nice man. He seemed fine to me, and his land was right up against the beach where there were otters, seals and whales and horses wandering by. Nothing wrong with that! I stayed there about ten days and painted a rock circle for her. How she loved it but she wanted to be sure I hadn't painted one for that nephew of hers.

I visited Isabel almost daily and did errands for her. I was very surprised when she showed me that her money was in a coffee can under her bed, "Just in case you need some." I helped her bundle drying grasses for basket weaving. One of her granddaughters had tied up grasses with rubber bands. Isabel made it clear that they should be tied with a long blade of grass. How peaceful and companionable those hours of tying and drying grasses were. I was even invited to join the women in her family on the beach as they split grasses, sang, and baked fresh salmon tied to sticks over an open fire in the sand. I experienced then what's sometimes described as "the eternal moment," a sudden recognition of the continuing ancient outside the realm of linear time. That was a part of my experience in Green Grass too.

On one of those beautiful afternoons a photographer from Seattle named Jim Malecki, arrived to take pictures of our activities. Everyone knew and liked him because he had been gathering information about the Makahs and the life of Isabel in particular.

Jim knew the area well and took me to see some beautiful parts of the reservation. At sunset on one of the beaches there we saw that rare phenomenon, the green flash and shared a vision of a path and portal in the sea inviting us into another world. What if we had followed this vision? We will always wonder! Visions can be shared. In fact, I think they may exist on a plane of reality that is only sometimes visible to us. When I told Galen about the spider web of light around the planet which so moved me, he said, "Ya, I seen that one." I wonder how many people shared it; did it a have a specific origin outside the mind of the beholder?

I saw Jim Malecki again in Seattle where he was just opening an art gallery he named, "The Summer Song Gallery." "Hey, could you paint one of your rock circles for us for Earth Day?" And that is how I had a show at Summer Song Gallery in April '95 and gave my performance, "How On Earth I Found a Voice." And returned there at the end of the summer to tell those stories again after the beautiful time I had in Haida Gwaii.

Saying goodbye to Isabel was hard. I said I'd try to come back for her 100th birthday. It was only a few years off. I'll always remember her face at that moment I said goodbye. She seemed not to believe that I was really leaving. I hardly believed it myself because I felt so at home there.

It was hard to remember why I had been so desolate on arriving at Neah Bay now that its beautiful world had embraced me. Again, as in Medicine Lodge, it was as though the place had been waiting for me. I believe I experienced these crises of confidence because I was so distant from my home in NYC and so far ideologically from my culture, living as I was, on the rarified air of spiritual inspiration. Sometimes it was hard to sustain my faith in what I was doing and as a small woman I sometimes felt physically vulnerable, especially in the unfamiliar woods or open spaces. I guess I occasionally longed for some kind of reassurance. I told Joan Pancoe that I was "working for the unseen." While a bear spirit or an eagle spirit might manifest now and then, we couldn't really sit down and have a chat. I mentioned to a friend I couldn't imagine both sides of a conversation with the "unseen." A few days later, I received a set of Jamie Sam's, and David Carson's, *Medicine Cards,* with their beautiful animal images and messages. Those cards really helped. In fact, it eventually seemed that the "unseen" wanted to chat almost as much as I did. I reminded myself that as a studio painter I often felt I was not working alone. Who or what is the "Muse," artists of all kinds have talked about through the ages? I do wonder! The engagement in many arts like painting and writing is a solitary task. Is the Muse born from the artist's need for company or does solitude invite the Muse to participate? Perhaps both possibilities are true.

A few years later Jim Malecki told me that the Shaker minister in Neah Bay talked Isabel into getting rid of the rock circle I'd made for her and which she loved. "It isn't Christian," he said. My simple prayer and "thank you" for the wonderful life of earth was somehow threatening. My circles were not expressions for or against any religions whatsoever. They were personal "thank you" notes to the Earth from a grateful guest. Naturally I hoped that people who saw the circles felt some appreciation for the life represented on them or that they gave some thought to the life of the planet and their relationship to it.

When I was later commissioned to paint some rocks for a Catholic University on the east coast I was asked to explain in writing why a circle was part of my art. It made them uneasy probably because historically/traditionally Christianity viewed circles as a part of the nature-centered Pagan religions it believed must be banished.

The circle is imbued with mystery and power. It "speaks" to us because it mimics the sun, moon, the earth itself and the paths of the planets as well as the paths of electrons circling an atom. There is the circle of seasons, the circle of the Zodiac, the circle of monoliths at Stonehenge, the Aztec Calendar, the Rose Window at Rheims, the labyrinth at Chartres, the Tibetan Buddhist mandala of Kalachakra, the great Medicine Wheel in the Bighorn Mountains of Wyoming and so on. Through history around the world, diverse spiritual ways have found ways to express devotion to God, Creator, or Great Mystery through use of the circle.

In my work I am most concerned with the healing aspect of the circular form. Carl Jung used to encourage his emotionally distressed patients to draw mandalas, the Sanskrit word for circle, because the order imposed by the mandala form helped these patients to integrate the diverse and apparently conflicting elements in their lives. In the case of the animal rocks the circle imposes order on diverse pictorial elements so that the observer focuses not so much on a single image as on the concept of the whole, which concerns the animals of our planet and in the larger sense, life on Earth itself. If this idea is perceived, the observer may consider his relationship to it. Perhaps some resultant thought, emotion, or action will bring about greater harmony in our confused relationships with the natural world. This would be healing and is what I work for. Although observers may not respond as I hope, I believe the Earth herself feels the love and thanks these circles express from her grateful guest.

For that university I also wrote about the ancientness of painting on stone. Sometimes I felt mysteriously connected to those "prehistoric" artists though my illustrative style could in no way compare with their ecstatic drawings. And my painted rocks were not intended to endure but rather, like the sand paintings of the Navajos and those of Tibetan monks and others, return as prayer and love, to the Earth. I simply borrowed these stones to act as a medium for communicating love and gratitude. When I took them from the earth or a river, I gave a prayer of thanks with tobacco as Joe taught me.

I believed the stones carried my prayers, that they could feel them and that the earth could feel them. Although we can rarely hear or feel it, everything has a vibration because everything is alive in its spinning atoms. I had a real sensitivity to stones in my hands. They did not all feel the same. Some had humming vibrations, others pulsed, or felt like static. I never painted on both sides of the stones so they could more easily convey to the Earth the feelings I put into them and eventually return more easily to the Earth, their home.

Life After Martin High Bear

The next time I saw Martin High Bear he was in a coffin. I flew from New York to Rapid and I got a lowered last minute fare because I said I was going to the funeral of a family member. It felt that way. I rented a car and drove up to Eagle Butte for the funeral. This time I passed sorrowfully through that land I loved so well. I stayed in the motel owned by the intimidating white woman. While she and I were not exactly friends, there was now some bond of appreciation between us.

The funeral was held in the Cultural Center a day later. When I walked in I saw the coffin on a table at the side of the room and many rows of chairs. In the background I could see the women at work. They were cooking. I stood in the line to view Martin and say some final words to him. He lay in a simple pine box, packed with sage wearing his cowboy hat and aviator sunglasses. That was the look he favored. I looked down at him. I smiled. I couldn't think of anything to say to really express my feelings. All I could think to say was, "Have a good trip, Uncle Martin and thank you. Thank you for everything." Even in the diminished state of death he emitted a breath of that whirlwind energy that was him in life.

A traditional Lakota "Give away" concluded this gathering at the cultural center and it was a big one. I was given a nice blanket because I was the person who'd come the furthest. The giving away of possessions expresses gratitude and ensures a feeling of good will among the recipients informing the event. The donors know they will, at some time, be recipients. The "Give away" is a way of being on the reservation. It's a kind of fundamental poetry of life.

There was a feast of buffalo stew and we all sat around the coffin eating it, conversing and enjoying ourselves. There were speeches and they weren't all about Martin. It was a bit like a public forum. One woman stood up and said, "Whatta ya do when your medicine man marries a white woman?" This made some people uncomfortable because Martin was living with a white woman, and I know she did her best to take care of him, not an easy job! He was revered as a healer and teacher but known to be on the wild side. He was also the target of jealousy and hostility from many of his fellow tribesmen. Sadly, this is too often the case for those who become in some way successful.

I was so glad to see Grey Bear again. The morning before the funeral we drove out to Green Grass to pray at the Pipe House where the Calf Pipe is kept. It's such a tiny spot in the vast prairie but overflows with power. I was happy to see my painted stones were still near. As we meditated there, a hawk arrived and circled the Pipe House, dipping low, almost touching the ground before circling again. Many people said Martin was a shape shifter and that he most often appeared as a hawk. Grey Bear and I looked at each other and whispered "It's Martin. He's saying goodbye." Maybe he would circle around Bear Butte where he gave so many ceremonies. He used to say, "Yeah, I have a Ph.D., it's a Ph.D. in Bear Butte."

After the feast, speeches, and give-away, Martin's coffin was placed in the back of a pick-up. We all got in our cars and followed it down the road out of town until it turned into the prairie where we bounced along after it. There was nothing out there to suggest a cemetery or any kind of formal burial ground. Men got out with their shovels and dug the grave. The red sun was just sinking into the prairie as the attending medicine man, a young apprentice of Martin's, spoke his prayers in Lakota. As dirt was shoveled on top of the coffin and the last red light of the sun shone, he shouted, "You leave him be. He's gone. You don't speak his name no more." No one spoke his name for a year. His journey after life would not be interrupted by any of us.

We turned back to Eagle Butte where a number of us got tables at the steak house. Grey Bear and I sat together. I recognized friends of his from California and Nevada who had been very friendly at Martin's Sundance in Oregon but now seemed oddly cool.

During dinner I got up to go to the Ladies Room and when I returned, Grey Bear was not at the table. There was a commotion outside. There were police cars with flashing lights. I was dumbfounded to see Grey Bear being handcuffed. No one in the restaurant did a thing. They said nothing. I ran out and said, "What's going on here?" Grey Bear said he was accused of selling an artifact important to the tribe. It seemed like everyone present must have known about it. Not a word was said. I looked around at blank faces of people with whom I had once shared a special time. I paid for my dinner and walked across the street to the motel.

Next morning, I went to the jail to see him. Telling Grey Bear he looked good in prison orange failed to cheer him up. The charges were soon dropped as mysteriously as they were made, and he was released after a week. I still don't know the real story behind his arrest. Maybe nobody does. I did what I could for him then drove to Bear Butte and to Blackhawk to see Joanie. I got on the plane in Rapid City for NYC and while eating some soup one of my front teeth fell out. Grey Bear's brother-in-law died suddenly from a heart attack in the same time span. I wish I knew what else transpired then. It felt like Martin High Bear's spirit was on the warpath. Or there was a serious trickster at work.

Toward the end of Martin's life when he was hospitalized with emphysema, Grey Bear made a video of him speaking to an audience in the hospital about healing. He told how the gift of healing usually skips a generation, that his grandfather had been a healer and the gift was passed to him. It was sad to see Martin so diminished but when he started to speak about healing plants, I saw his face become magnified, just as it had at the Sun Dance. Grey Bear said many people had the same experience when Martin spoke of an aspect of healing that was personally important for them. It was like a last gift from this great medicine man. It's true that healing plants were becoming a strong presence in my life. Grey Bear asked if my painting of sage plants standing against a prairie sky could be used as the cover for this video. Well, of course!

Yellow Horse And The Gathering Of Eagles

I was now deeply committed to my vision and to the spiritual ways of tribal people who have not forgotten the Earth. I now understood the importance and value of ceremony and the necessity of listening to Life in its many manifestations. I felt comfortable with myself as a person who had visions and usually felt confident that Spirit was there to guide. And I was having the adventure of a lifetime! With Grey Bear as my adventure guide, I met a constellation of special people and participated in unique events that did not, thankfully, include sudden police arrest during dinner.

The communication system known as the Native American Telegraph is astonishingly effective. Grey Bear seemed to be a major destination on this line of communications and he was kind enough to allow information to spill over in my direction.

One early spring morning I heard a raspy voice on my answering machine. It announced there would be an Intertribal Gathering of Elders in June near Custer, South Dakota. Here was another invitation Native American style, nothing specific in it, nothing to cause feelings of obligation. Like a puzzle, I confess I enjoyed the challenge of solving it. Neutral information is considered more polite and also implies the recipient must have enough focus to pursue the details. If you couldn't figure it out, you weren't meant to be there anyway.

A couple of days later a message declared that Chief Yellow Horse would be installing a medicine wheel during the elders gathering and that anyone interested could bring a stone to add to it. I could hardly wait, elders from different tribes AND a medicine wheel AND all of that occurring in the Black Hills with its handsome buffalo herd, and the old log cabin home of that great prairie poet Badger Clark AND near Bear Butte as well! I was looking forward to my idea of heaven. Patience and a few phone calls soon cleared up the questions of time and place, almost.

I left my cabin on the Snake, always leaving a part of my heart there, though remembering the best part about leaving, was knowing I would be returning. I drove across Nebraska to enter the Black Hills as Eric and I had done in the year of the Harmonic Convergence. I stopped to give a tobacco offering in that place at the edge of the Black Hills where I believed I had found "my people" after a long separation. I had a vision there, a man, clearly Native American, rose from the earth and leaned toward me.

Suddenly it started to rain and became torrential. I drove on very slowly until I had to stop. The road was a river. I was scared but then a deer emerged from the sheets of rain and stood in the road in front of me. It stared at me for a long time and I met its gaze. It was as though I was being asked to please remember the Black Hills are a sacred destination. They have always been sacred to the Sioux and would have been a part of my experience in that old life of mine. Humbled and thoughtful, I continued and arrived a few days before the gathering.

Good that I arrived early since the location of the gathering had changed and I had to find it. I parked in a Custer State Park campground for a couple of nights. The intense aroma of pine trees and the music made by wind flowing through them makes me feel drunk. But I wasn't drunk when I saw a rabbit with three ears hop through my campsite. Like Alice, I wanted to follow it, imagining it might lead me to other worlds but I remained content with the sense that unusual things might be in store without having to do that.

The stone I brought to be included in the Chief Yellow Horse medicine wheel was one I'd found in Russia, on the banks of the Volga in Nizhni Novgorod. I was fortunate to find it. It had markings that suggested cuneiform and I felt it could be translated if I only knew how. I later painted a portrait of this stone as a kind of mandala with a yellow horse running through it. The last of my oil paintings were pictures of individual stones. While I painted on stones I was also painting pictures of them. You could say I was "stoned!"

At the appointed hour, Yellow Horse, a tough wiry old gentleman, led about twenty of us up into the hills to a small grassy plateau donated by a local family for his medicine wheel. What I'd forgotten until then was there had just been an international gathering of tribal people in Brazil. It was called the "Earth Summit." It was led by the United Nations in June, 1992 to discuss pollution, global warming, and many issues that continue to concern the world. That explained why there were individuals from the Philippines, Australia, Alaska and Mexico, Japan, Korea, and the West Indies present with stones in their hands. How had they found their way from Brazil to Custer South Dakota? The mysterious Indian telegraph had been busy!

We asked each other, did we bring the stones together for this medicine wheel or did the stones bring us together for this, a worldwide prayer in the heart of the North American continent? Yellow Horse smoked his Pipe and sang the prayers and we, a group of strangers from around the world, were joined by wonder, gratitude, and love in a moment so empowering it felt there was no problem in the world we could not solve.

For three days, elders from different nations spoke and ceremonies were conducted in what became known as "A Gathering of Eagles." Many said this gathering was the true "Earth Summit," which, by the way, the President of the USA chose to ignore.

An elder in a Native American gathering is always acknowledged with respect. It is assumed that the experience of long life has provided you with some valuable or helpful insights or at the very least some darn good stories. You are not ignored, but treated politely. To equate "elder" with "eagle" was a declaration of the high esteem in which older people are held. Eagles are, for so many indigenous people worldwide, messengers of the Divine.

Personally I suspect there is a bit of eagle in my DNA. After all, it was the vision of an eagle that brought me to Bear Butte to see the beautiful web of stars. It was an eagle, the African Fishing Eagle, that broke my heart open to singing in a way that has now become a form of healing and prayer. Appearances of eagles at certain times always indicated to me that I was going in the right direction or was in a safe place. I do feel real kinship with them and indeed, all the winged ones. Maybe it began when I was twelve years old visiting a roadside "zoo" where the owner invited me into the cage of a bald eagle. He lifted up the eagle and placed it on my skinny arm. I still have the memory of its weight and talons in that arm. Its name was "Sam."

And there, in the middle of the "Gathering of Eagles," was Grey Bear "running sweats." His Sweat Lodge ceremonies were magical. Once again I sang a song for water in one of them and I knew it was beautiful but couldn't remember it to sing again. Other people in that ceremony asked for it, but as always, those songs from the heart are only for the moment. In that same Sweat Grandmother Spider made an appearance in a web of light at the top of the lodge that was witnessed by all and there were spirit lights aplenty! When we finally emerged, soaking, from the lodge, it was night and we were told there had been a big thunderstorm. Never heard a thing. We had been in there an unbelievable three hours! Where had we been transported?

While tribal elders of the world were exchanging ideas, knowledge, problems and solutions, many having to do with the care and preservation of the Earth, the ministers in the pulpits of Custer's churches warned their congregations away from the dangerous heathens on their outskirts!

In attending gatherings like this, hosting Pipe Ceremonies in my home, acknowledging the power of eagles and other species, was I "playing Indian?" Was I an Indian "wannabee?" Was I becoming an Indian? No, most definitely not. I was in fact, becoming myself. I was recovering my true humanity, the humanity I was seeking behind the barriers of a materialistically driven culture, a culture that regards Earth as "resources" for the acquirement of power and money, a culture that does not want to admit we are but one species in a large Earth family all of whose members must, at the very least, be respected.

Perhaps the desire to communicate with our Earth family is inherent in our nature and we mourn its loss. Perhaps we have buried reverence for our planet and its life but have become helpless to define it or afraid to express it. Fortunately, there are still some remaining indigenous people who feel at home on the earth, comfortable in their relationships with other earth denizens, and have not forgotten how to express reverence in meaningful ways. And importantly, some are willing to share their knowledge with us who are deprived of what was once normal for all humanity.

Chieftains On Appaloosas

Just how threatening Native Americans were, and still believed to be by authorities, was a shock to me. Helicopters and trucks full of soldiers arrived at Devil's Tower, Wyoming during an extraordinary ceremony I had the good fortune to attend. Did they imagine some kind of "Indian uprising" might take place? It was, in fact, a homecoming ceremony for descendants of bands of Lakota who fled at the turn of the last century and made their way to safety in Canada. They returned on horseback. They rode the many miles from Canada to Devil's Tower. I was taking a walk around the outskirts of the area where they were to congregate. Quite by accident I was one of only a few to witness that breathtaking moment when they began to appear almost magically, one by one, from the forest astride their gorgeous Appaloosas. It seemed a dream or that they could be spirits from the past. They sat straight and high wearing their long trailing eagle feather bonnets, fringed deerskin jackets and leggings. They carried shields and eagle feather staffs. They were magnificent. They were the very images of the "Indian Chief" known by people around the world. Seeing them emerge from the forest in full regalia was a powerful vision of their past splendor. Even though these men were no longer lords of the land, they exuded the true power of real dignity. Oh, I regretted not having a camera but was so accustomed to not using one on ceremonial occasions I'd left it in the van.

Arvol Looking Horse was present, and the very old chief of the great Crazy Dog Society and other chieftains. The already buzzing campground at Devil's Tower was suddenly thrown into intense commotion when the word arrived these great Native men would bless our Pipes. We all rushed to comb hair, straighten clothing and be presentable. We, the assembled Pipe holders walked to a large open area in the shadow of that immense rock core of a former volcano. To me, Devil's Tower looked again like a giant crystal, with each of its "facets" the width of a boxcar. As we assembled in a large circle holding our Pipe bags, I looked around and saw a few familiar faces from Green Grass among the Canadian Lakotas.

My Pipe bag was made for me by Grey Bear from blue Pendleton wool and had a beaded medicine wheel sewn into it. Many Pipe bags were fringed hide with porcupine quill embroidery or beading. We were asked to fill our Pipes. I think most of us were experiencing some amount of disbelief that this could be occurring. It was too amazing. Then, one by one we approached Arvol and the other leaders, Pipes in hand. The suffering etched into the faces of some of these old gentlemen whose people had lost so much, gripped my heart and as usual, near Arvol, I tripped and nearly staggered into them all. I even heard Arvol murmur some excuse for me to the others. So embarrassing.

After all the Pipes had been blessed, we were invited to remain and smoke them and share them with one another. The sharing of Pipes also occurred at Sundances. I was always very moved by this sharing and the sense of deep community it gave. The soldier-filled trucks soon left, having made their point, but I doubted they understood what had taken place.

A year later, the hosts of this ceremony at Devil's Tower rode north into Canada, sealing the circle of family and comradeship, or as Arvol would say, "mending the hoop."

Keeping A Promise

Galen Drapeau was one of the unusual people I met through Grey Bear. He was and still is a great healer. When Joanie in Blackhawk phoned to say she had been diagnosed with ovarian cancer I called Galen right away. I asked him if there was anything he could do. He replied that he was leading a vision quest at Bear Butte and I could bring her along at the conclusion of it. One of the vision seekers was a young man named Francis. He had gone to the Museum of the American Indian in New York looking for a spiritual teacher and was sent to my apartment on 85th Street. Lucky for him it happened to be the New Moon, that day when there was always a Pipe Ceremony in my home, and that Galen was visiting and conducting the ceremony. That fortunate kid became Galen's apprentice and now, here he was on the slopes of Bear Butte coming down from his first Vision Quest.

One by one the participants arrived, looking tired but full of wonder. Joanie and I were allowed to hear their accounts. One woman was kept company by the spirit of an Indian woman dressed in skins, who looked normal, except that her feet didn't touch the ground. Francis reported that a snake had entered his altar and licked his Pipe. Galen told him to give his Pipe to me, a Pipe with the transformative powers of Snake! And that is how I received a Pipe larger than the one Mona had given me.

Joanie was given a star quilt and moccasins, all blessed by being on the mountain for four days and nights. Then Galen started to pray and asked all present to pray for Joanie. As we stood around him, we watched a small cloud work its way up the mountainside, growing larger as it came. Suddenly a bolt of lightning shot down from it and struck the ground very close to us, making all of us jump a foot in the air. It seemed to have a voice. Galen didn't flinch, just said he was pleased because the lightning had spoken his Lakota name.

Joanie is still cancer free and enjoying her grandchildren twenty years later. While she did receive some traditional cancer treatments, we believe the healing power summoned by Galen was the turnaround.

During the visit to Galen's home before my Hanbleyca, I promised to paint a rock circle for him and his family on my return journey, not knowing then what a long journey it would be. After the vision quest on Bear Butte I drove on to Medford, Oregon with Grey Bear for Martin High Bear's Sundance and then wandered north, painting circles up the coast to Neah Bay at the tip of the Olympic Peninsula. After a brief visit to Seattle I began driving east. Somewhere on that stretch of road I stopped at a campground that didn't have an available space but the owner said I could park "down by the lake." I parked there not knowing I was in for a memorable night of stargazing. I hadn't known the Pleiades meteor shower would be at its peak on this date. What a display it was, all those shooting stars flying across the heavens reflected in the lake for a glorious light show. I didn't believe I was just "lucky" to experience beauty such as this, but blessed.

Continuing east I drove across the northern part of Idaho. I was warned this area was not friendly to people other than the clearly white middleclass. A friend in NYC joked that the best way to travel through that part of Idaho was with a set of golf clubs highly visible in the back window. A small city was on my route and as soon as I entered it a police car attached itself to me and followed me closely until I was out of town. Didn't know I was so dangerous. Of course I had a medicine wheel hanging from the rearview mirror, bunches of sage and turkey feathers hanging from hooks in the side windows and a "Turn In Poachers" sticker in the back window—clearly not the kind of person northern Idaho welcomes. I'm proud of it.

I was headed for the Big Belt Mountains in Montana where the daughter of a friend was working for an Outfitter and I planned to meet up with my newly married daughter and her husband in Bozeman where he was showing her the sights of his birthplace. When my daughter peered into the back of my van noting the feathers, bundles of sage and grasses, assorted rattles, Indian carpet and weaving under my typewriter, a small deerskin, a buffalo hide bundle, a small cactus plant, jars of paint and books of drawings she said, "Mom this is just like your apartment in New York, just smaller. I like the way you arranged those rocks with your sleeping bag in the middle." She is an artist and would necessarily take note of how the interior of my van was "designed." We had a nice lunch in a restaurant. Then they drove west and I continued east hoping to reach the famous Crow Fair in the Crow Agency before it began.

Coming along the road I could see a hillside filled with tipis. I had no idea it would be like this. I came to the turnoff to go up there and was stopped. The women there said it was full up but looked at me again and decided I could probably find a place to squeeze in. They were right but it wasn't easy. I no sooner parked and opened the door to take a stretch when a little boy holding the reins of his horse came running up to me, "Please help me, Miss, I can't get up on him." I gave him a big boost onto a very tall horse. There were horses everywhere. I'd always heard the Crows were "horse people" and so they seemed. That little boy said he was riding to the rodeo. I went on foot between horses and smiled nonstop at all those people on horses outside the rodeo ring watching more people on horses inside the ring.

Wandering around the encampment, looking at tipis, being greeted by friendly people from different tribes in between horses felt like heaven. I decided I had to paint a rock circle here. I did have those nicely "arranged" stones in the van. But those were supposed to be for the circle I'd promised Galen. Oh well, I could find some more.

I put my cooler outside and used it as a table for painting and I sat on the floor in the doorway of the van. It worked well. Very soon I had the curious and charming company of some young children. They were mostly concerned about where I would take these painted stones. What would I do with them? They were so excited when I said I would leave them in the clearing where we were so they could always visit them. Such a happy time! It even included a tiny bit of romance when a handsome and well-known Navajo mural painter from Flagstaff discovered my van "encampment." His special spirit shone from his eyes. At the end of the fair he said he didn't understand why I wasn't following him down to Arizona, and I said I didn't understand it either. Reluctantly ending an embrace, we parted and drove off in different directions. A hard moment of longing, of imagining shared joys of the road, the great pleasurable adventure of getting to know a beautiful soul and the possibility of love.

During the fair families had reunions, celebrations, and ceremonies because their relatives and friends from other tribes were gathered there. On a walk one day, wishing I had some money to buy some of the stunning handicrafts for sale, I came to a large open area where people were gathered in a circle. At the far end a beautiful Crow girl appeared in her buckskin dance regalia fringed with elk's teeth. On each side of her were three of her tall, handsome male relatives, their arms linked together. Their pride was palpable. They were presenting their cherished daughter/niece/sister. They danced slowly around the circle. Their strong presence made it clear this girl was protected and must be respected. They threw candy to the children at the edges of the circle and threw coins to other onlookers. They were making the statement that they were rich and generous, a very fine family and that only suitors of status would be of interest. Those men were declaring they wanted only the very best for this splendid young woman.

Well, I did break down and bought a beaded deer bone, an object of sweet beauty reminding me always of my many meetings with members of the deer family and the wonderful Crow Fair.

My journey continued. Before long I was across South Dakota approaching the Southeast corner where Galen lived and I realized I didn't have the rocks I needed to fulfill my promise to him and his family. I studied my map and didn't see any promising sites for the smooth river rocks I needed. I was tired. It was a long summer of driving. Behind the wheel I cried out loud, "I am so tired I don't know what to do! Help me please. Please help me find my stones." I suddenly realized I was not on the route I had planned. I must have made a wrong turn. I was lost and then almost immediately there was a sign announcing a rock quarry. Couldn't believe my eyes! I zoomed up the road and right away saw a pile of stones that were perfect. I got out of the car and walked in farther and was met by a big tough stone-wall of a guy. I blurted out that I was an artist and that I needed some stones to paint for a project. He stood there, hands on his hips scowling at me. I held my breath. Finally, he said, almost shouting, "You can take what you want for a dollar. But you are not supposed to be in here!" All the way down the road I sang my thanks to those spirits who pitied me and led me in my tired state to this unlikely place.

I couldn't find a campground nearby so I stayed in a motel in Yankton where the owner simply assumed I was visiting someone in the prison there and smiled indulgently when I tried to explain the rock circle I began to prepare. When it was ready I was more than happy to "hit the road" again.

On the way to Galen's I saw the tribal casino down the road and since I was feeling really good I dared to try my luck and decided to stop there. In I went straight to the slot machines and right away won a jackpot of over three hundred dollars, just what I had paid for food for Galen's family on my way to Bear Butte for the Hanbleyca! Well now, doesn't it pay to keep your promises to your friends and to the art that speaks your heart? And knowing I was mightily blessed I left immediately with my winnings and drove off feeling victorious to Galen's house where no one was at home. They had left for a ceremony.

I placed the stones next to my van and fell asleep until I heard knocking on the windows, the excited laughter of children, and Galen's voice calling "Claire, Claire!" What a happy moment! I felt welcome and at home.

Pyramids And A Sacred Hawk

Another exciting opportunity to travel arose again, this time to Egypt. Once more prices plummeted because of political unrest. This time it was terrorist activity.

On my return from Egypt I was stunned when Galen called me in New York from South Dakota to tell me he was going Egypt. I started to babble excitedly, "Oh you must go to the pyramids and meet Champion. He's kind of raggedy looking . . . but he can let you into the pyramid at night and," "Claire, Claire, slow down, I'm going to Egypt to do a ceremony for him!" My reply was a gasping, "What, how can that be?"

Apparently Francis, that young man I'd first met at a ceremony in my home and later, after his Hanbleyca on Bear Butte, had gone to Egypt and met Champion, perhaps the same way I had, as a guide for the pyramids. Because Champion's health was failing, Francis contacted Galen. Champion was so named, because he was fastest climbing to the top of the great pyramid when he was a kid. That's what kids did for fun there when he was young!

I met Champion when I arrived at the ticket booth for the pyramids. I was approached, at first, by a well attired, haughty-looking Arab, who offered to be my guide. Then a ragged, one-eyed, Arab–pixie popped up and said, "I'll take you. I know what you want!" I chose him because I could see that he wasn't trying to impress me but intuitively understood I was on a quest, not someone wanting more photos for the family album. He led me away and took me down some unmarked steps into the ground. There he pulled out a large key to open an iron gate. It was the tomb of the mother of Cheops. We entered and when he turned on the lights I burst into tears because standing in front of me were life-size statues of a group of women all smiling, standing with their arms around one another. Through my tears I gulped, "These are my sisters from another time." It was a shock, a wonderful one. I wanted to embrace them and left reluctantly. Champion was my champ! He even offered to open the great pyramid for me so I could spend a night inside it but I was on a tour and didn't think I could get away with that and also I thought it was too scary for me.

Galen, on his return from Egypt, reported he'd done a ceremony for Champion out in the desert and that rain had come. Galen told me that he was "pleased." I imagined Champion's health was restored. Often there are years between rainfalls in the Sahara.

The small tour I joined in Egypt was led by a young Australian woman who got us up at dawn and to every site of interest before the crowd. We were fortunate. When we sailed up the Nile we bunked on a small native boat and could stop to talk and walk with people on the banks. At one pause in our journey I left the boat to take a walk and sat to rest against a sandy bank. Suddenly I felt something crawling up my back. I jumped up, looked down and saw that it was a large beetle. A member of the crew summoned by my shriek, told me it was the dung beetle sacred to the old Egyptians who connected it with the transformative powers of the sun god. I had seen it many times in the ancient art of Egypt where it was called a Scarab but was unaware of its interesting origins. The crew on the boat said I had been blessed by its visit. So it wasn't just a big bug that startled me but the sacred Egyptian scarab bringing me the good fortune of having met a famous inhabitant of the ancient Nile Valley.

We docked at the town of Edfu and climbed a steep ramp up to the long riverside esplanade where eager crowds offered guide service or things for sale. A pleasant young man, a student strolled along with us. He mentioned in abbreviated English that he was unable to find an English/Arabic dictionary. I promised to send one if I could find it and took his address. Later I received a nice note of thanks and felt happy I could repay his brief kindness to us on the far banks of the Nile.

At the end of the esplanade in Edfu we were driven a short way into the desert. There stood the great temple of Horus the Hawk, lord of the skies, manifested by pharaoh on earth. It was perfectly preserved because it had been buried in sand for centuries. The temple entrance is flanked by two enormous statues of Horus, wearing the crowns of upper and lower Egypt. These monumental statues emanated such power and dignity it was easy to imagine flinging myself on the ground before them.

Each year at midsummer, a statue of Hathor, the cow eared goddess of love, music, and childbirth, left her nearby temple in Dendera to sail up river in her sacred barque to

Edfu. Her statue would be adorned in finest regalia and accompanied by her priestesses and celebrants. I imagined wonderful singing and music taking place as she arrived in Edfu to be met by a statue of Horus and his priests and celebrants. Following a grand procession, the two divinities would then retire to the temple for a month while everyone celebrated their union. A cow-eared goddess and a hawk god might seem like an odd couple, but their union represented the coming together of heaven and earth making the joy associated with it understandable. To this day, Edfu is called the "The Town of the Beautiful Meeting."

Guidebooks claimed there were carved reliefs in the temple depicting these festivities and I was eager to have real visual descriptions of this momentous union. Adding further zest to my interest was the fact that I, with another woman on the tour, managed to see the temple of Hathor, in Dendera, which was off limits to visitors because of random terrorist activity. We were in Luxor a few days before boarding our boat for Edfu and on a free day we snuck off like naughty schoolgirls. We persuaded a very reluctant cab driver to take us there, draped our heads in dark scarves and wore large sunglasses to disguise our western appearance. We succeeded in exploring Hathor's home from rooftop to bat filled basement. Most intriguing was a ceremony of women going on in one of its chapels. It was clear they didn't want us or anyone else to see them.

Once inside the temple of Horus at Edfu I hoped to locate the reliefs depicting the festival of "The Beautiful Meeting." Soon I was crouching in a side corridor inspecting a relief I thought might be what I was looking for. I was interrupted by a temple guard who wore the turban and frayed, dusty galabeya, the long, wide-sleeved shirt-like garment of the Arabs. When I looked up at him he beckoned to me. When I said something about Hathor and Horus he just nodded. I checked my pockets to be sure I had enough "baksheesh" the tip money that so many people depend on in Egypt, then followed him to a staircase where he pointed up to a magnificent carving of Horus, with wings outspread. There was a small window opposite and somehow I understood that this glorious carving would be alive with light at the solstice, possibly at the time of Horus' meeting with Hathor. The widespread wings reminded me of the confined eagle, "Mon Coeur" and I nodded appreciatively.

He led me to the back of the temple where, in an alcove, there was an elaborate wooden model of a barque clearly relating to this ceremony. I had a strong sensation of music. Then by way of explanation, this odd man pointed to the barque, flung open his arms and started to chant. I knew he was attempting to convey the essence of this ceremony of union, joyful hymns. How exciting! To show I understood, I responded by opening my arms and I sang something from my heart as I now did so often, but the sounds that flew out were unfamiliar. Though different, they seemed linked to the chant I had just heard. It was as though we'd mysteriously recognized one another because without a pause or word, he grabbed my hand and ran, pulling me along a corridor on the other side of the temple to a small chamber.

He pointed to an opening in the wall that was above my head and indicated that I should go up there. I shook my head, gesturing that I could not fly. He looked around, checking that no one was present, cupped his hands in a stirrup and, as if in trance, I stepped right into it. He catapulted me up to the opening and somehow followed me. Only as I crouched in the narrow dark passage inside the wall, did I feel a bit frightened. At the end of the passage were some pieces of cardboard to sit on and some bowls for incense. This man said, or I should say, ordered, "You sing here!" I did sing while simultaneously trying not to think, "no one will ever find me here." What spirit was I singing to or for? When I finished singing we descended after he checked the chamber below was still empty.

Once again he tightly grabbed my hand, this time pulling me to the main altar, an immense standing slab of granite. He pulled me through a group of babbling French tourists and shoved me behind the granite, put a bowl of burning incense between my feet, slapped my hands on the granite and commanded, "You pray here." When my hands and forehead pressed against the granite I got an electrical charge I'll never forget! Horus had blessed this poor fool follower of Hathor, me.

I was nearly overcome but clung to the granite and gave thanks to the spirit for acknowledging me. Dazed, I wandered out to find this man and to thank him. We stood, holding each other's arms looked intently into each other's eyes and nodded. I gave him the ring I wore then and all the baksheesh.

How I wanted to know what ceremonies from times past continued in the secret chambers of the temple of Horus. And how I wished I knew the name of my guide into the past or his address or how to fully communicate, but I guess our singing/chanting voices expressed what was most important.

When she saw me wander distractedly out of the temple, that lovely young Australian tour leader Catherine said, "You look a bit wonky, Claire. You all right?" I smiled and asked her if some of the spiritual ways of ancient Egypt continued in some places. She replied, "There are rumors."

Singing On The Nile

Our next stop on the Nile was one of the islands in Aswan where we dropped our luggage at a somewhat luxurious hotel. It was hard to say goodbye to our very nice crew but the next boat was waiting, a felucca with its wide white sail, to take us to the west bank where camels awaited us.

With Catherine as our guide we had designated free times but outside those, not a moment was wasted. I was enthralled by the movement of the felucca that glided so rhythmically over the fast moving eddying waters of the Nile. I started to sing and later the boatman, a Nubian, thanked me for singing on his boat. He said I had blessed it.

The rhythm of a camel was quite different and I enjoyed it too. We passed a dwelling where a female camel was giving birth and her cries were heart breaking. We rode up onto cliffs to see rock-cut tombs, then into the desert to visit an old monastery and last, the mausoleum of the Aga Khan, a very big man who used to give his weight in gold and precious stones to his followers on his birthday. Nobody suggested he should go on a diet.

We returned to the felucca and were taken to an island with a sound and light show and then, utterly exhausted, we were dropped off at a Nubian village on Elephantine Island where a dinner had been prepared for us. Our hosts, all men, (as it's not proper for the women to show themselves), served us a meal of fish, beef, salad, rice and beans, and Coca-Cola with abundant good will. We, however, sat like zombies struggling to stay awake in the candlelight. Hospitality in Egypt is not a casual thing and I felt badly we were so unresponsive to this unusual dinner. So, as we were leaving the mud brick home of our hosts, (and hostesses who giggled and peered at us through cracks in the wall) I stifled yawns and said rather boldly, "You have been so kind to us I would like to sing a song for you. It is the song of a little river, not like yours, and children like to hear it." I sang a song that had, one morning, come from the Snake River, "Wey Hey ho ho ho ho, Wey hey ho weya weya weya Ho...."

Wow, the energy of the moment flipped. These men ran for their drums, held them over a fire on the beach to make them tauter and started to sing and to dance. Soon everyone joined in. We got on one of their boats and sailed around still drumming, singing, and dancing under the stars. When our collective exaltation peaked, our wonderful hosts sang their love song to the Nile, to its seasons, birds, and fishes. It became so quiet then it seemed the river itself was listening.

Among Native people it is accepted that a spirit of nature can bless you with the gift of a song. I received a song from the mist in Oregon, from the Snake River in Nebraska, and it was an eagle that opened my heart to song. When visiting Neah Bay, a Makah woman honored me by singing a song that had been "given" to her. I gave the Snake River song to a Paiute drummer from Nevada when he asked for it, and I gave it to a village on the Amazon, and now I had "given" it to the Nubian musicians on the Nile. In all cases I was asked for the use of the song and thanked for the gift of it. How splendid it is to connect with others in this way, through song, that language the Earth shares with all of us.

A song, given by a spirit, is a treasured and respected gift.

Egypt for me, was another visit to the "eternal moment," always strange, always familiar, always mind-blowing. In experiencing those moments I knew I had lived many times, and I had a sure sense of myself as an earth being who was connected to all others throughout time and in the present. In those moments, which occurred more frequently as I journeyed the Earth's great rivers, I felt an ineffable peace.

Star Ships And Magical Manataka

At the conclusion of the Vision Quest on Bear Butte that became a healing ceremony for Joanie, Galen said to me, "I think you better come to the Star Knowledge Conference out in Lake Andes." "Okay, Galen," I said very light heartedly, "if you think I should," not knowing as usual, what I was getting into but believing it might be the kind of opportunity my heart always sought. And of course, I trusted Galen. His, was a voice of authority that I loved.

I agreed to drive Francis to the Conference and feed him after his four day fast on Bear Butte. We headed for the Badlands and spent a night there watching a glorious prairie lightning display.

The Star Knowledge Conference was held in a school auditorium. After a day of listening to Native speakers talk about space ship landings, the Star Nations, and ceremonies connected with constellations as defined by the Lakota, my sense of the "real" world was expanding. I felt uneasy.

Before sunset, Galen, who had just arrived, asked the assembly to stand out of doors in a circle and to hold hands for a prayer. As he prayed, little clouds arrived and soon formed a complete circle directly above our circle. Dear Galen, a man forced into Indian Boarding School as a child and damaged by Agent Orange in Vietnam, grew such a big heart that even the clouds love him. We occasionally joked about how there were always clouds hovering above his house.

Along with other people from the Conference I parked my van in a campground along the Missouri River that night. I crawled into my sleeping bag, and Francis pitched a small tent behind the van. At some point during the night I was awakened by a voice commanding me to "Look at Venus!" At the time, Venus was unusually close to the Earth. I was aware of that and had seen its powerful beauty on several nights, so half asleep I grumbled, "I've already seen it." But then I quickly sat up realizing that it must be a spirit that had spoken and looked out the window to gaze upon that magnificent planet. As I did so, there was a stunning explosion of light in the sky just beneath it. Then lights began gliding back and forth above the hills on the opposite bank of the river. People in the campground were shouting "UFOs, UFOs" and coyotes were howling wildly.

I got out of the van shaking from head to foot and could barely speak as I tried to absorb this. But I woke up Francis so he could see them too. Were they beings from beyond the sphere of Earth that had come to greet us in response to the Star Knowledge Conference? I think so, but adjusting to the actuality of visitors from outer space was difficult. I wanted to believe in them and was simultaneously afraid to. To Frances their arrival seemed perfectly natural. He tried to connect with their cerebral vibrations through meditation. I have a feeling that Galen knew this might occur.

Next day as Francis left to join Galen, he turned to me and said, "I hear eagles practically throw their feathers at you." My most treasured compliment.

If not for Grey Bear, my life would not have been honored by the presence of Galen nor would I have met that splendid man Lee Standing Bear, a chief of the Cherokee and leader of Manataka.

Because of those welcoming people in Medicine Lodge Kansas, I was determined to see the Peace Treaty celebration that occurred there every two years in September. They were eager for me to attend this event and I looked forward to seeing them again.

I set off from Athens, Georgia where I was visiting my daughter Deirdre and her family. I now had a Roadtrek, a most wonderful vehicle complete with kitchen, toilet, bed, storage, and only sixteen feet long. It was a Canadian vehicle created from a Dodge Ram. The part of me that loved dollhouses truly cherished this van. I had first seen one in a campground out on the Queen Charlotte Islands, (Haida Gwaii) in British Columbia. I stood in front of it then, hungrily examining its details until the door opened and a very tolerant couple invited me in to take a look. Later that year my former sister-in-law, riding a train from Montpelier to White River, Vermont spotted a Roadtrek in a used van lot, sent her partner to check it out and we bought it within hours. No more sleeping bags on the floor of a rented van, though truthfully, I sometimes missed traveling that way.

In a phone conversation with Grey Bear I mentioned I was heading out to Medicine

Lodge to attend the Peace Treaty celebration and he insisted I go to Hot Springs, Arkansas to meet his friend, Lee Standing Bear. I really wasn't enthusiastic about detouring from my planned route so I just said I would try. But I knew I'd do it. After two days of driving I pulled into a campground in Hot Springs tired and grouchy but I called Lee Standing Bear and left a message in a somewhat surly tone of voice. "This is Claire, a friend of Grey Bear I'll be in this campground until ten tomorrow morning." How ungracious I must have sounded. I'm embarrassed to remember it. Next morning there was a knock on my little door and there stood a very tall, handsome, (wow!) Cherokee! We sat at a picnic table and I had enough presence to make some coffee.

Bear, as he asked to be called, had brought his Pipe bag and laid it out on the table. It was heavily fringed and he straightened it out little by little as he began relating the story of Manataka to me in his wonderfully resonant voice. He described the old Hot Springs, how rainbows leapt and hovered in the mists rising from the many healing springs in the hills. Artifacts from the Inuit of Canada and Mayans of Mexico, were found there, demonstrating that the healing powers of the springs were known far and wide. I was entranced by the world he conjured.

Manataka itself was a huge intertribal ceremony, shared even by traditional enemies. All weapons were laid aside. It was known as the "Place of Peace." The climax of the ceremony came after hours of dancing when suddenly everyone was able to speak the same language, and this, Bear said, was why they came, to share this extraordinary moment of primal connectedness. I wept at the wonder of it. What a storyteller that Bear is! Before leaving he gave me a spirited quartz crystal, which always accompanies me. And to think I had nearly passed up the opportunity to meet this incredible man and be touched by the magic of Manataka, both the place and the ceremony. Nowadays, Manataka is also an organization which supports Native culture, provides ceremony, and a number of services.

The remainder of my journey was filled with sights of poignant beauty—unusual cloud formations, rainbows, and the sight of migrating geese mingling with colorful pheasants on the red and yellow floor of an autumn forest lightly dusted with snow. The magic of Manataka was with me. And my return to Medicine Lodge was a pleasure.

When, in 2001, I was caught up in the tragedy of "9/11" and my plane returning to New York from Indonesia was forced to land in Halifax, I remembered Bear and Manataka. The plane came from Asia, traversed through Europe, carrying an assortment of people who resembled my granddaughter's dolls of the world collection, different costumes, colors, religions, and languages. Suddenly, housed in a school gymnasium, we all spoke the same language, the primal language of compassion. It was a revelation. Love and compassion live deeply within all of us and connect us all. How splendid it would be if we could just remember it.

Chumash And Speaking Stones

*I*fled a cold New York winter and flew out to California to visit my newly married daughter, Deirdre and her husband Jim, living on a charming walk street in Venice. Both are artists and both were preparing work for important gallery shows. I felt happy and proud and glad to do the cooking!

The beach in Venice is full of colorful life both human and a multitude of other species. I relished my walks there listening to the music of the sea. On the pier in Santa Monica I saw someone selling abalone shells. I love these swirling rainbow shells. I bought all of them for a "give away." They are used in ceremony for the burning of sage and they remind me of the vision that I had on my Hanbleyca, of all life spinning into a rainbow in the bowl of my Pipe.

One afternoon while wandering at the water's edge, dodging waves, picking up pebbles, and shells, I snatched up a small bland looking stone before it was engulfed by a wave and automatically turned it over to see what was on the other side. What a shock! A tiny tiger's face glowered at me. It was animated. It's little jaw opening in a silent roar. Absurdly I gasped, "What are you doing in there?" I had learned from indigenous people that stones are spirited, and I felt that myself, but nothing I knew could have prepared me for this! I have felt different vibrations from stones but this was such a specific vision. I threw it down as though it were too hot to handle, walked away, then turned around, picked it up again and put it in my pocket. What could it mean? Maybe it meant I was losing my mind! I looked at that stone repeatedly but the little tiger did not return.

While I was in Venice, Grey Bear called. Both he and I were often on the West Coast and met up when possible. We had a shared interest in rock paintings and carvings, and had talked in the past about someday seeing the rock paintings of the Chumash in the Santa Barbara area. This seemed to be our chance since we were both in the same place at the same time. I said I'd rent a car so we could drive north to Santa Barbara.

The only car available was expensive because it had a phone. Who needs a phone?

I'd driven all over the continent without one. I was annoyed to be paying for something I regarded as superfluous but that was that. I said goodbye to Deirdre and Jim and said I'd return in two days. Grey Bear and I drove off and on the way when I described the tiger stone to him he just laughed. "Supernatural" occurrences are a "natural" part of life as far as he and other Native friends were concerned. And truthfully, the supernatural was becoming more a normal part of my life too, but I always found its manifestations surprising.

Once in Santa Barbara, Grey Bear and I headed for the museum to learn more about the Chumash, a people who had lived in the extraordinary abundance of the coast in that area. We were directed to some small caves in the hills above Santa Barbara where we saw, through heavy iron bars, the intensely colorful paintings of the Chumash. Most appeared to record or describe astronomical events like eclipses or comets. Though defaced, they were still stunning. But the presence of iron bars made them sad.

Later in the day we found rooms on the fifth floor of an old wooden hotel in the center of town where the price, this time, was right. Early next morning we headed out to the Carrizo Plain where there is a large site of Chumash rock paintings.

It was much further than we thought and our directions were muddled. On a funky back road that suggested we were truly lost, a truck bounding toward us honked insistently. We all stopped. They had spotted the medicine wheel hanging from the rear view mirror. They were a group of Native Americans working for Wallace High Elk and of course they knew everybody Grey Bear knew and had relatives in common. It was old home week out there in the middle of nowhere—very Indian and I loved it, though I doubt the concept of "nowhere" is part of the indigenous psyche. They knew where we were headed and gave us accurate directions. We hadn't known the Nature Conservancy was the caretaker for this site and finally pulled into the parking lot of their visitor center at four o'clock. The Center was closing but we were told we could walk to the rock site about two miles away. We went as fast as we could because the sun was just hovering above the western mountains.

"Awesome," that word which seems to have been invented in California where people say everything is "aaawesum" really is the right word for this dark circular rock formation that rises from the flat expanse of the valley. Big black rocks stand in a nearly closed ring—maybe the eroded core of an ancient volcano. Grey Bear and I entered the circle, the only people there, and looked across the wide circumference to the tallest of the rocks, about a story high. Once inside, the whole circle suggested a giant head with sloping shoulders tapering down to a space between hands where we had entered. We walked into this embrace and ran around looking under ledges and into cavities to see the Chumash paintings, calling to each other. "Oh, this looks like a space ship . . .I think this is a comet." It seemed to us the Chumash might have recorded celestial events and ceremonies connected with them here. After the Star Knowledge Conference with Galen it no longer seemed fanciful to imagine the arrival of star ships.

Grey Bear, who is always ready for a ceremony, had his Pipe with him and said we must smoke the Pipe in this clearly sacred place. He was disturbed that there had probably not been a ceremony here for a very long time and I strongly agreed. Traveling with him was always a trip, so to speak. Any nook or cranny of the earth like a spring, or special looking rock that might have received ceremonial attention in days gone by, is acknowledged by Grey Bear. He is determined to make up for lost time in honoring these manifestations of the Earth's energy.

Well, he loaded his Pipe with tobacco and we began to sing the Pipe song, standing there in the middle of this big stone circle. "KOLA LECHE LECU OY." We sang it four times to honor the four directions, and as we sang, the coyotes began to sing with us. They seemed to be singing in a circle on the outside and they were getting closer and closer. Grey Bear and I smiled at each other. Then we began the song that specifically honors the four directions. These are the songs essential to the Pipe Ceremony. As we began this song a fox suddenly appeared. It ran along the rock ledges with elegant light-footed grace.

And then, the rocks began to move! They became animated. The ledges and cavities appeared to be stretching to form features that were yawning and grimacing. For a terrifying moment it appeared monsters surrounded us. Grey Bear and I did not move. Our feet were firmly rooted in place on the solid unmoving earth beneath us. We were literally stunned by what we were witnessing. A wide-eyed look shot between us conveying the message, "Don't move, don't dare stop singing, keep going." As we were concluding the song, the enlivened rocks subsided. We smoked the Pipe with shaking hands and ran for it. It was easy for me, at least, to imagine that stone embrace might close in on us. It was getting dark. What else might occur I couldn't imagine. Although accustomed to the belief that all nature is spirited, this was certainly outside the range of our collective experience! Could it be, we wondered, that the earth had wordlessly spoken to us, that it was enlivened by this ancient ceremony it had missed for so long. Or maybe, like the coyotes, it just wanted to sing along.

It was late when we got back to Santa Barbara and we were ravenously hungry. The only restaurant open after ten o'clock was a 50's-style diner where Elvis Presley's voice rang out from the jukebox, singing, "I'm All Shook Up," and that is exactly what happened at four in the morning. A terrific earthquake!

I jumped up, ran to the doorway of my room as my earthquake-smart California daughters had trained me to do. I could see Grey Bear down the corridor clutching his Pipe, his mouth open and eyes blinking. A naked woman dashed out from the room across the hall but was pulled back and then the lights went out. I imagined this old hotel had stood through many quakes but I feared it might be the last time, it swung so far. Just as I was saying goodbye to the world, it stopped. I grabbed my things, Grey Bear was there in a flash and we ran down five flights of stairs in light thankfully provided by a generator. We ran to the car, grateful now for its once despised phone! I called my daughter in Venice to be sure she was alive. She told me the road back had fallen into the sea and we'd better head up to San Francisco to the home of my unaffected daughter. I called her to tell her "refugees are on the way."

Before leaving Venice, I had painted a small group of stones intended for a part of Santa Barbara where the Monarch butterflies winter. The center stone was a butterfly. It was an area threatened with development. That dear man, Grey Bear, helped me place the rocks in a circle even though the earth seemed to shift slightly now and then under our feet. When the butterfly stone was placed in the center of the circle a sunbeam spotlighted it and a Monarch butterfly landed upon it. Once I understood that Spirit speaks in these ways I never felt alone though I was often in very lonely places.

It seemed clear now, that the little "tiger stone" was announcing a coming earthquake as did, so dramatically, the circular rock formation of the Chumash site. Grey Bear said the Pipe Ceremony helped the Earth to be more comfortable during an adjustment her body needed to make. And I wondered if all stones or rocks can become vividly animated under certain but unknowable circumstances other than impending earthquakes.

Stones
You are my pathway to the stars
My bridge across rivers of time
Trail maps discarded by the past
Puzzle pieces of the world

You are my adventure books
My lucky charms
Handheld buddies
Amusing and kindly teachers
Surprising me at every turn in the road
Lying sphinxlike at intersections
Impossibly patient
Sunk in wry humor
Or wisdom ancient and profound

What imagining can decipher your heart,
Comprehend the urgency of your molecular essence
When in a moment you change vibrations
To speak
To become a moving visage?

O trickster story stones
I wait for you
I listen, I watch
Hold my breath
Prepare to greet you
With a pinch of tobacco
Cornmeal, a penny
Or a song will do
To speak my heart's gratitude

For the feel of you in my hand
The way you awaken my blood to sing
Enliven my heart for adventure
Press me to pray
Engage me in play
Affirm I still walk the pathway to stars
My spirited stone companions
My star-born friends.

How surprised and pleased I was when eight years later my granddaughter, the divine Lucy, visited my little forest home in Georgia and on seeing the lovely stone wall there exclaimed with joy, "Gaga, (her name for me) these rocks have feelings; they have spirits!" It seemed wonderful that she was naturally receptive to the life and vibration of the stones and further, that she expressed it. I had a small basket of crystals and said, "Oh Lucy, let's put these in the wall so the stones know how much we appreciate them." What followed was nearly an orgy of gift giving. The nooks and crannies of the wall were soon filled with crystals, seashells, mosses, flowers, and messages of love! And of course, thanks were given with pinches of tobacco too.

Lucy was only a few months old when Rosy conducted a Name Giving ceremony for her in the garden behind my apartment on 85th Street. Many friends gathered and all those who smoked the Pipe with us at the New Moon each month. The Four Directions were called upon. A little breeze arrived. Rosy looked up and declared with a smile that Lucy's Indian name was, "Singing Sunflower." Sitting on her mother's lap, Lucy received the gift of a wish from each of the guests. She seemed to listen intently. This was followed by a Pipe Ceremony, in which her father touched her with the Pipe. She seemed perfectly at ease throughout. Now she is in her twenties and already a prize-winning poet, true to her Indian name. I don't think she will forget that stones have spirits.

The name given by Rosy to my younger granddaughter, Gwen, was "Crystal Mountain Rose." She is psychic with a deep respect for the animal kingdom. Very casually one afternoon Rosy gave me her look that zaps you and said, "You could be called, 'Woman of Many Medicines.'" Grey Bear sometimes called me, "Blue Rock Woman" and Chief Chris Leith, who I sometimes met on Bear Butte with his dear family called me, "She

Puts Herself Up." This name refers to the fact that after learning the requirements for a Hanbleyca, I performed some of them myself when spending a night on the mountain.

Many children intuitively feel the spiritedness of nature but, to the detriment of the world, are made to abandon their natural feelings. Those childhood memories that I most like to revisit are imbued with feelings of how "special" was the toad living in tree roots, the flicker in the tree, the blossoms in tulip trees, the turtle laying its eggs, owlets in a hollow tree, the cry of a kingfisher, the robin's evening song, the annual explosion of gnats, visits of ladybugs, the thrill of the Milky Way.

Now, it is my joy to give a pinch of tobacco or song to acknowledge gifts such as these. Fortunately, my childhood summers were on a lake in the country. I wish all children could spend time among the glories of nature and feel the love of their planet.

Cultures devoted to the acquirement of material goods seem to find it inconvenient, or even absurd to respect the spirited and sacred Earth.

Pink Dolphins And Green Ice Floes

As Joan Pancoe had predicted, my journeys spiraled out from the continent. It began in 1990 when the presence of Shining Path guerrillas along the Amazon in Peru lowered the cost of tours in that region. A group of friends grabbed this opportunity usually unaffordable to us as artists. My daughter Madeleine joined because she had written a book for children entitled, "Here is the Tropical Rainforest."

We flew into Iquitos, were herded into an old bus that shook and rattled through the forest. In a magical moment we passed an open pavilion alive with lights, pulsing music and dancing people, a colorful smudge against the darkness, before continuing along silent unlighted streets. It was like a dream and the perfect preface for all that followed.

We stayed briefly at a place on the edge of the forest, met amusing monkeys, and importantly learned never to wander off any given path and to be very wary of touching anything. Then we boarded a small riverboat aptly named "The Arca" with Daniel as our splendid guide. He was a man with a doctorate but without work in his discipline. He was the best of guides because his keen knowledge of the land and its people was informed by his love for them. He made the casual but astute remark that America is the only place where people look down on you if you are poor. Most people in the world are poor.

The entire journey seemed a dream. Some of us swam in the river with bright pink dolphins, while others fished for piranhas on the opposite side of the boat. We stared unbelieving at giant lily pads that could hold up a child, gorgeous macaws that erupted from the jungle, at the armies of leaf cutting ants, grasshoppers big enough to be leashed as pets for village children, pet monkeys that swung in miniature hammocks. We heard the great cry of the "horned screamer" a bird with claws at the joints of its wings that was a relic of the age of dinosaurs, gazed at huge fishes, experienced the great kindness of village people, and so on and on. A tour of wonders! Fortunately, my former sister-in-law, Jane Walker Richmond the photographer, was present and knew how to capture the magic of the place.

Toward the end of our journey a handful of us moved into a small riverboat, really a long outboard with a roof. One night as we were about to sleep on the boat's narrow benches, someone came out of the forest to tell us men of the Shining Path were near. We quietly hiked inland to a little house on stilts where we slept on tiny mats much too small for our large North American bodies that pressed against the diminutive mosquito nets surrounding the mats. We avoided the guerrillas but one of us counted more than two hundred mosquito bites on one arm and during the night I felt a hot needle penetrate my butt. It was a scorpion. For three days I had hot flashes in my derriere. It was like repeatedly backing into a hot stove and I would jerk forward, amusing my daughter and friends no end.

I couldn't paint rocks in this flooded muddy world but I had brought a stone from Bear Butte. I placed it, wrapped in red cloth, at the point where the Ucayali and Maranon Rivers meet to form the Amazon. I sang for the energy of the mountain and rivers to meet and gave tobacco. Now it was a part of the web I was spinning.

Further down river I left a large amethyst given to us by someone from the Native American community in NYC. He sent it as a healing gift to the continuously threatened rainforest. It was especially blessed because we had rescued a python from some boys in a village and released that elegant snake as the amethyst was placed on the earth. How profoundly beautiful it was to see this handsome creature recover itself, move to a tree, and sinuously wind around it as it climbed, before wrapping around a high branch where it observed us from safety. It was an occasion for singing. All of life is sacred. How deeply I felt it here where the web of life is a dense pulsing fabric of myriad interdependent species all clamoring for life. More and more I felt a pressing need to celebrate the ineffable wonder of creation by singing.

A different kind of singing could be heard in the jungle on that night we spent in the stilt house where the mosquitos were so numerous and so voracious we were forced to get under the mosquito netting before 6 o'clock. It was too early to sleep so we entertained ourselves by singing camp songs. We were far from the river, the jungle was noisy with its own songs, but we sang softly, just in case. "There Was a Farmer had a Dog and Bingo

Was his Name-O" was one of the songs we sang. We insisted we had summoned the gods of Bingo when Madeleine later won a game of Bingo on the return flight from Iquitos to Miami. We claimed the victory had to be shared and Madeleine, coerced into seeing reason, treated us to glasses of champagne from the bottle she had won.

In profound contrast to the jungles of the Amazon was the frozen world of the Canadian High Arctic. In late summer 1994 a voyage Jane Richmond and I planned to take to the fjords of Norway was cancelled. We were asked, "Would you mind going to the High Arctic on a Russian ice cutter?" Wow, wouldn't mind a bit! And so my journeys "spiraled out" again, this time to the top of the world where the earth in deep silent thought dreams creation. In my journal I wrote, "I see the pattern for a butterfly's wing etched in the side of an Arctic mountain." In Native American teachings I received, North was considered to be the direction that emanates wisdom. A scientist on board the ice cutter described it as the place where past and present meet to create the future. There is evidence that many species of plants and animals migrated south from the Arctic.

We flew from Toronto to Resolute. It was doubtful we would be able to land the fog was so thick. Peering out the plane window we didn't see the gravel runway until we were on it. We were bussed to a school where we received certificates stating we had crossed the Arctic Circle.

Curious children surrounded us. I gave them little woven "friendship bracelets" from Peru and showed them my book of rock circle photos. Then I asked them to help me find stones because I wanted to paint a rock circle in the Arctic. Very soon a stack of stones appeared in front of the school and were bussed to the beach where more were added to await transport by zodiac to our ship, the Klebnikov. During the wait a very special elderly gentleman named Jim Miller became interested in my project and helped out. Jim and I and the stones were on the last zodiac for the ship and inched our way up ladders to the decks above while the Russian crew made jokes about stones being brought on board.

Jim seemed to be the living embodiment of my goal to be as alive as possible. At age ninety he swam with whales, at eighty-eight, hitchhiked across country and got a job in a tuna-canning factory. He had friends everywhere. Tales of his fascinating life added a rich and unexpected dimension to the journey. He was a gift as were the "experts" on board who were a botanist, geologist, ornithologist, and historian. Instead of learning the names of trees and all that lived among them as we did in the Amazon, we learned the different aspects of ice: "new ice" can be frazil (crystals), grease (oily), shuga (larger crystals), nilas (sheet, and then there was "Young Ice," "First Year Ice," "Old Ice" and so on. Ice of "land origin" is icebergs and their relatives, "bergy bits" and "growlers," those parts of bergs not visible under water and not seen by radar. Gregorovich was the member of the crew who acted as ice observer and interpreter for this expedition. Experiencing a whole new landscape with its particular terminology was like learning a new language, or simply more of the language that describes the multiple facets of the Earth. I thought of the Hawaiian words that describe lava flows, Hopi words that express rain, Inuit words that define snow. Earth Woman's sparkly green sequins glowed fiercely.

The artist in me thrilled to the luminous blue/green of ice against dark water and the fluid forms of ice suggesting sculptures by Henry Moore or shapes in paintings by Miro, shapes that breathed life, like clouds become solid. The vistas with ribbons of fog and light moving through them were dreamlike. Polar bears occasionally loped across these scenes with astonishing light-footed grace. When I wasn't feeling spellbound, I was feverishly painting rocks in the spacious cabin I shared with Jane while she was avidly storing the Arctic world in her camera.

Part of the journey was going out in the zodiacs to visit bird rookeries or Inuit villages. We experienced a frisson of danger when surrounded by icy fog in a zodiac and were unable to locate our ship. And again when our ship was stuck on a sandbar and had to jettison much of its water supply. There were also helicopters on board to carry us to some sites and on one occasion to rescue passengers trapped in ice on a zodiac.

I had a stone from Bear Butte with me and imagined I would place it on Ellesmere Island where Dave Mech, the biologist, and Jim Brandenburg, the photographer, had studied and documented the lives of white wolves for *National Geographic*. I was in love with those wolves and hoped to see them but didn't. I did, however see an amazing moment in the life of the Arctic Hare. Every seventeen and a -half hours on the dot, the mother hare nurses her young. They arrive and suckle so eagerly that they lift her in the air and carry her along for a full minute, then leap and frolic with comic exuberance. Everything in the Arctic must mature quickly to survive because the period of sun and warmth is short. The vegetation is beautiful but miniature in size. How surprising it was to find a spider's food cocoon with a bumblebee inside it.

When transported by helicopter to a hilltop where there was a mummified forest perhaps fifty million years old, I could not contain the impulse to sing. Looking out there were dark layers of silt, like stripes, all representing the remains of ancient tropical forest. I picked up a "freeze dried" fern. It crumbled in my hands. And as it turned to dust, my heart was gripped by knowing the huge holiness of the Earth. Here I sang the Lakota song that honors the four directions. As I did so, the continuous wind stopped blowing until I finished singing. I placed the stone from Bear Butte here. It was wrapped in sage and red string. I gave a tobacco offering which seemed such a small way to express the love and gratitude I felt. A strong vision followed: a glowing, shimmering, electric blue waterfall descending from the Arctic to revitalize the Earth.

At the end of this journey, my painted stone circle was transported by helicopter to Resolute for the school. I hope those great kids who contributed rocks enjoyed it. A year later I had the pleasure of painting a circle at "Ten Bears Farm," Jim Miller's place in Ohio. He was that grand gentleman who helped me, a stranger, lug rocks from an Arctic shore aboard the Klebnikov. In a dream at the top of the world I heard, "The universe trusts you with its abundance and you love every moment of the sharing."

My web spun out to Asia in 1997. The world of Bali captured me. Now I live there half the year on a small farm in the mountains at the edge of the jungle. There I enjoy the company and magic of many children, animals, and spirits of the land.

The mastery of skills necessary to survive in any culture is so challenging it's hardly surprising the primal understanding of the divine in life we are born with recedes from our conscious minds. Some cultures, however, strive through story, song, art, and ceremony to access the primal knowledge that connects us all to each other, to all that lives on our planet, to the divine, and to all that spins in the universe. Balinese culture is one of these. Materialistically focused cultures and power-ridden religions discount or strive to eradicate, often ruthlessly, any such understanding. They rob us of the splendor of true humanness.

In the ten years recounted in this memoir, the Earth asked me to remember I was her child and I ran into her arms. I accepted Joe's eagle feather and remembered a lifetime when I understood gratitude and how to express it. I became unafraid to be taught by ancient spirits of wolf, bear, eagle, spider, and mountain. As best I could, I honored the visions I received and have tried to remain faithful to them. I saw that everything is imbued with spirit. I learned to be braver. I learned the value of ceremony. I learned I am never alone. In being as fully alive as possible, I attempted to honor the dead. I received the precious gifts of heart singing and healing hands to love the living. In the stars I saw that all is connected and learned the "eternal moment" is now. I spun my web of painted stone circles and sung my love into them. Most importantly I learned that Joe was right, expressing gratitude does make your life better. It makes everything better!

Did the Earth, beloved Gaia, feel the love in my songs, the love from my hands as I painted animals and stars on her stones? Did she feel the pulse of love in the web that I, one of her small creatures spun? Did the sacred mountain smile? Did a few stars chuckle? Bronx Apache Rosy would give a short hard stare with raised eyebrows and nodding quickly say, "Yeah, ...oh yeah."

And I became CLAIRE EARTHWOMAN. Color me sparkle glitter green!

Claire L. Dunphy

I felt compelled to write this memoir of ten years. Without the patient and cogent guidance of Mark Leichliter of the Wordwright, it would not have been possible. Thank you, Mark for the joy of communicating this adventure. You are a great teacher.

Many thanks to Hannelore Hahn founder of the Intrernational Women Writers Guild who insisted long ago that I could and should write, and to Dale Carlson of Bick Publishing House, for years of encouraging my many artistic endeavors. Thank you, Jan for your unwavering enthusiasm for this book. You kept me writing to the end. As part of The Tribe, a gathering of artists and healers in Athens, Ga., I am grateful to Christy Gray, our guide, for her inspiration and wisdom.

Thank you Jane, for your adventurous spirit and superlative photography.

Thanks to TJDD, a generous patron.

Heartfelt gratitude to Bill and Bowen of Bilbo Books Publishing, the finest of companions in the publishing process. They along with Dan Roth of Athens Creative Design have happily actualized this book from my wandering years.

Thank you, Eric for helping me on my way.

And thanks, at all times to friends everywhere who encourage and care.

CPSIA information can be obtained
at www.ICGtesting.com
Printed in the USA
FSHW012100230319

9 781732 618022